TIKTOK MARKETING FOR VIRAL SALES

A YOUNG GIRL'S GUIDE TO BLOWING CUSTOMERS' MINDS

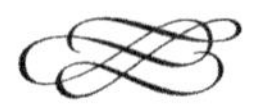

ANASTASIA OLSON

ISBN 978-1-7362482-1-8

CONTENTS

11 Suprising Hacks to Grow Your Brand on TikTok v

Introduction vii

Chapter One: Is TikTok Right for Your Business? 1

Chapter Two: Creating A Perfect Tiktok Profile 18

Chapter Three: How to Make Great Videos on TikTok 37

Chapter Four: How to Grow Your Account 57

Chapter Five: How to Get the Most Out of TikTok 66

Chapter Six: Reach Your Customers Through TikTok Ads 77

Chapter Seven: Working with TikTok Influencers 105

Conclusion 121

Also by Anastasia Olson 125

11 Suprising Hacks to Grow Your Brand on TikTok 127

References 129

11 SUPRISING HACKS TO GROW YOUR BRAND ON TIKTOK

(NEVER START A TIKTOK WITHOUT THIS...)

To receive those steps, visit the link:

http://book2climb.com/TikTokSuprisingHacks

INTRODUCTION

> *"Imperfection is beauty, madness is genius and it's better to be absolutely ridiculous than absolutely boring."*
>
> — MARILYN MONROE

Everything you have been told about going viral on TikTok is probably a lie.

On the 13th of July 2019, a TikTok user named Reese Hardy posted a video of herself crying and dancing to Mariah Carey's 2009 song, *Obsessed.* What should have been a routine TikTok video instead blew up the internet and became one of the most viral sensations of 2019. It became known as the #Obsessed Challenge and was adopted by millions of people all over the world. So, how did Reese Hardy pull it off? How did a video depicting a crying girl dancing to one of the less commanding Mariah Carey songs become the love of the internet (Corry, 2019)?

Bella Ciao! Very few memes and challenges have gone as viral as 'Bella Ciao' in 2020. There was the Bella Ciao dance challenge, which dominated TikTok for months. The Bella Ciao hair clipping challenge was even more interesting. It was essentially a challenge to make a hair bun with a pencil, mimicking the style of inspector Raquel Murillo in the popular *Money Heist* TV series. A closer study of this challenge raised a burning question within me. How does a century-year-old Italian revolutionary song become such a social media phenomenon? Undoubtedly, the popularity of Money Heist played a considerable role in this. Still, there have been other songs on many exciting TV series, which are just as good and arguably more modern that did not have such an impact on TikTok. And there have also been far more exciting scenes from *the Money Heist* TV series, which never went as viral as the hair clip. So why does a bland, inconspicuous hair clip worn by a police inspector in a Spanish TV series go viral (Chon, 2020)?

The two examples above made me begin questioning everything I knew about marketing on TikTok. What exactly pushes ideas or actions from the relative simplicity of people's bedrooms to dominating on TikTok? Is there something you have to do to significantly increase your chances of going viral? And what precisely distinguishes viral content on TikTok from non-viral ones, which are just as good, or even better?

At age 16, my Dad brought home a vending machine asked me: "Do you want to start a business?" I responded positively, and by the time I graduated high school, I had acquired a few other vending machines, which contributed to my college fund. This was a great bonding experience for my family, and owning those vending machines at a young age provided me with so many skills. I learned everything from how to start a business to business management and expansion. It also looked so darn good on my CV and on every application I've ever submitted. This is my biggest motivation for writing this book.

After graduating from the university where I studied marketing, social media, and entrepreneurship, I sold my vending machine business to an 11-year-old girl. I became her mentor, assisting her through the process of becoming a successful entrepreneur. These skills and experiences have fueled my passion for this book. I consider TikTok a place where every young girl can aspire to start their own businesses with the help of a mentoring book. This book was written after months of poring through all the available data and information about thriving on TikTok. I analyzed years of viral videos, memes, challenges, and accounts to compile a holistic and easy-to-apply method to become better at TikTok marketing.

I became passionate about writing this book not just because I majored in marketing/social media in college or because I started a business at sixteen. I became passionate about it because I know TikTok is not just the future of social media, but also the future of marketing. This, coupled with my passion for mentoring, has been my driving force throughout the difficult process of writing this book. Nothing would make me happier than to motivate young girls to become successful entrepreneurs through TikTok. That is why this book is different from every other type of book. It passionately provides an excellent understanding of almost every area of TikTok. It covers everything from lighting quality for videos to deciding what hashtags to use and what challenges to participate in. My simple goal is for you to become more successful on TikTok. This has the power to potentially improve your self-confidence, creativity, and provide opportunities for you to earn more money.

With billions of downloads about two years into its creation – excluding the years of Musical.ly, TikTok has become the fastest growing social media app in the world and one of the most popular mobile apps in general. In 2018 and 2019 alone, the app was the most downloaded on Apple's App Store, surpassing other major apps like YouTube, Instagram, Facebook, and Snapchat. TikTok is particularly dominant with teenagers and Generation Z, and it has done more to raise creative influencers than probably any app in history (Al-Heeti, 2020).

If you already use TikTok, you might have invested a lot of time and effort into creating videos and participating in challenges, with the hope of increasing your likes and followers. But did they increase as much as you wanted? My guess is, despite most people's best efforts to look cool and as funny, they are still struggling to move the needle in any significant way. And because you can only accept donations on TikTok if you surpass the 1000 follower mark, becoming popular has literally become a race for the money.

With this book, I am presenting an entirely new way of understanding and creating viral content, using vivid examples and real-life scenarios from people who have been successful using these strategies. Although geared towards teenagers, this book can help anyone interested in thriving in the world's fastest-growing social media platform.

While the book might be useful for academics, it is not written for academic purposes but as a guide to help ordinary people realize their ambitions. Moreover, a lot of what the book contains could seem counterintuitive and fall in the face of conventional wisdom. It often goes against many of the TikTok marketing 'secrets' available on the internet – from YouTube videos to blogs. But I guarantee these revelations will work if followed correctly.

The first four chapters of this book explore the history of TikTok and everything you need to create excellent content. It explains how you can film exceptional videos, how to use hashtags and participate in challenges/trends, how to select songs/sound clips for your videos and how to write your bio and post descriptions. It also explores the equipment you might need, including providing tips for purchasing cheap lighting equipment and how to hire freelancers to design your company logo or profile image on TikTok. The next four chapters go deeper into TikTok marketing, exploring how to reach a wider audience with your uploads and how to use TikTok for your business. It covers topics like TikTok pro and how to access the data associated with your account, including your number of views, the reach of your posts, the gender/location of your viewers, and your number of likes, shares, and comments, among others. Furthermore, it also explores issues like how to become verified on TikTok, how to create viral ad campaigns, and how to work with TikTok influencers and micro-influencers.

But why should you care about TikTok marketing? Why should you continue reading this book? You should because from all available evidence, TikTok appears likely to dominate social media for the next decade, similar to the impact Facebook and Instagram had on the previous decade. If you don't have to believe me, believe Evan Spiegel, the founder and Chief Executive Officer of Snapchat. When asked about the possibility of TikTok dethroning Instagram in the future, he responded: "I think it's certainly possible because this talent-based content is often more interesting than status-based content." He had earlier explained how TikTok was different from other social media platforms because it wasn't about "showing people that you're cool, getting likes and comments" but instead about "learning a new dance or think(sic) about a funny new creative way to tell a story." Mr. Spiegel certainly has every reason sound less than optimistic about TikTok because his company is a direct rival. But in a rare moment of honesty from a true avant-garde of mobile technology, we can learn about the future of social media. If CEOs of rival companies expect TikTok to dominate the future, it most likely will.

This book contains everything you need to prepare you for that future. And for the present, of course.

CHAPTER ONE: IS TIKTOK RIGHT FOR YOUR BUSINESS?

"Do what is right, not what is easy nor what is popular."

— **ROY T. BENNETT**

IN AUGUST 2014, MUSICAL.LY WAS OFFICIALLY LAUNCHED as an app for creating 15-second to 1-minute lip-syncing music videos. It was also possible to choose soundtracks, adjust speeds, and add filters/effects to the music videos. By May 2017, Musical.ly had garnered over 100 million active users. Its success was primarily due to its ability to empower young people (Mohsin, 2020) to create uniquely viral content via hashtags and trending songs (Influencer Marketing, 2020).

At the same time Musical.ly was taking off around the world, a separate Chinese company, ByteDance, launched Douyin for the Chinese market in 2016. It instantly became a sensation with over 100 million users and 1 billion daily views within the first year of launching. By August 2018, ByteDance merged with Muscial.ly to create TikTok. It operated by separating Douying, which operates for the Chinese market, and TikTok, which serves foreign markets. All content and accounts on Musical.ly were automatically transferred to the new Tik Tok app, and like Muiscal.ly, TikTok was also based on the same short-form video concept. It soon, however, expanded its offerings beyond short lip-sync videos (Influencer Marketing, 2020)

TikTok is a social media app that enables people to create videos about music, dance, challenges, magic tricks, and comedy, among others. The main difference between TikTok and its predecessor – Musical.ly – is that with TikTok, there is almost no limit to the kind of videos that can be created, as long as it meets the app's policy. It has unleashed an unbelievable storm of creativity around the world, something New York Times TV critic James Poniewozik described as follows: TikTok "wasn't, like Instagram, trying to persuade me of its users' happiness, or, like Twitter, of their rightness. Instead the vibe is: Look at this cool thing I did. What can you do?"(Poniewozik, 2019)

Since its launch, TikTok has become one of the most popular mobile apps of all time. It was the most downloaded app on Apple's app store in 2018 and 2019, and according to the influencer magazine hub, it has the highest follower engagement rate of any app on the planet. By August 2020, TikTok had surpassed 1 billion downloads, less than four years after its creation, making it one of the fastest mobile apps to achieve this feat. (Influencer Magazine, 2020)

WHY HAS TIKTOK BECOME SO POPULAR?

1. Uniqueness:

According to John Holdridge, the CEO of social media consultancy giant, Fullscreen: "TikTok's success can simply be attributed to how it flips what we think of as social media on its head, while at the same time returning us all to roots of the original appeal–the ability to go viral. We've all gotten so caught up in maximizing reach by growing a massive fan base through subscribers or followers, so it's refreshing to have a platform with an algorithm that rewards content above all else. Because of that, it's pushing meme culture to new heights, giving Gen Z a visible place to be themselves while allowing brands to inspire their fans in authentic, entertaining ways."(Taulli, 2020)

2. Ease of use:

TikTok is by far one of the easiest social media apps in the world. When asked about it, Kenny Trinh, the Managing Editor of Netbooknews, summarized it as follows: "It's far easier to edit and upload content in TikTok than in other apps such as Instagram or Snapchat. Anyone with a smartphone can easily create and post content" (Taulli, 2020). It makes a massive difference, especially to young people, that an app provides a way to upload easily, edit, watch, and share videos.

3. People's love for Music:

According to Gregory Galant of Shorty Awards, "A key element to the app's success is the love of music by all age groups. The tie-in offers a fun twist that lends itself to new trends, memes, and challenges and with a steady stream of new songs constantly being released, there's always something new to do, a new dance, a new joke, etc." (Taulli, 2020)

Furthermore, Dmitry Shapiro, CEO, and Co-Founder of GoMeta alluded to TikTok's ability to inspire music remixes by popular stars. He explained that what "TikTok has really proven is that 'remixing' is the future of creation. It makes compelling content accessible to more people—and each trending remix on TikTok's platform only inspires more people to create. While original content is powerful, remixing gives ordinary people the power to layer context and self-expression and share within memes and discourse. TikTok is only the beginning when it comes to remixing's potential today." (Taulli, 2020).

4. Addictive Algorithm:

TikTok boasts one of the most addictive algorithms of any app on the planet. New York Times Critic-at-Large, Amanda Hess describes it as an app that does not default to "content from people you have chosen to follow but to content the algorithm has chosen for you. This has made it the only platform for which the term "algorithm" has, for me, a positive connotation." (Hess, 2019). She further compares TikTok to other social media like Instagram and Twitter, writing that the timeline algorithms on "Instagram and Twitter breed suspicion that looser, messier posts are being hidden from view, obscured by carefully framed announcements of engagements and jobs, pregnancies and euthanized pets. These platforms operate with a brittle predictability. But TikTok deals in the illusion, at least, of revelation. Even if all I'm doing is tapping my screen, "discovering" new videos has the feel of an internet treasure hunt." (Hess, 2019).

5. Celebrity Endorsements and Marketing:

Jimmy Fallon was an early adopter of TikTok. His interest grew naturally but was capitalized upon by the app through paid partnership. In November 2018, he launched the #TumbleweedChallenge challenge section on his TV show and used TikTok as the platform for the challenge. The challenge involved people posting videos of themselves on TikTok rolling like a tumbleweed.

TikTok has since developed partnerships with other celebrities and sporting institutions, such as the National Football League (NFL). Many other celebrities like Justin Bieber, Jennifer Lopez, and Will Smith, have also joined the platform (Hills, 2020)

6. Ability to create new internet celebrities:

No other app in the world can claim to have the power to create new internet stars like TikTok. Its unique ability to make viral content makes it possible for anyone to become famous overnight. The list of people who've become stars via TikTok is nearly endless. Among others, Lil Nas X's Old Town Road became the longest-running number-one song in the history of the Billboard Hot 100 after initially going viral on TikTok. Lizzo and Megan Thee Stallion, Doja Cat, and Melanie Martinez are famous people whose songs became popular through TikTok.

Apart from these celebrities, other people to become viral via TikTok include Loren gray, Zach King, Kristen Hancher, Lisa and Lena, Charli D'Amelio, Avani Gregg, Chase Hudson, and Addison Rae, among many others (Leskin, 2020).

WHY YOU SHOULD CARE ABOUT TIKTOK

1. The Biggest Marketing Opportunity in the World

Suppose you've got a special talent – like singing or dancing, or a knack for business, or you like to entertain people, or you're simply trying to find your path in life. In that case, TikTok provides you with an unprecedented opportunity to reach new audiences and markets without leaving the comfort of your bedroom. There has never been a bigger opportunity for more original marketing in history. TikTok's marketing clout has become remarkable, such that Bloomberg news recently dubbed it the "New Music Kingmaker".(Shaw, 2020)

Here are a few success stories:

i. Fitz and the Tantrums: This American indie pop band was founded in Los Angeles in 2008. The band's most popular song is *Handclap,* which was released in 2016. However, something strange happened two years after the song's release. By April 2018, *Handclap* was topping the music charts in South Korea, a country none of the band members had ever visited. The song also went viral in China, surpassing over 1 billion streams in 2018. How did they achieve this? TikTok! The song went viral in many Asian countries after TikTok users uploaded videos set to the song (Shaw, 2020).

ii. "Old Town Road" by Lil Nas X: Old Town Road was initially released on TikTok by Lil Nas X. He promoted the song by making it into a meme, which was eventually adopted by hundreds of thousands of TikTok users. The meme depicted people drinking some "yee yee juice," which transforms them into cowboys. This turned the song into a global sensation.

By the end of 2019, Old Town Road had become the most successful song of all time on the Billboard Hot 100, topping the charts for over 19 consecutive weeks. It also topped music charts in countries like Australia, New Zealand, Germany, Norway, and the United Kingdom (Strapagiel, 2019).

iii. Zombies, Run!: this is an Android and iOS app that helps transform the running/exercising experience for people, regardless of location. How does it work? You get on the app and run, walk or jog anywhere in the world. Then you receive your mission and music via your headphone, and you must increase your speed if zombies are chasing you. Early in 2020, a TikTok user made a post about the app, which instantly caught fire (Carless, 2020). The app's creators received so much traffic that it nearly crashed the company's servers, prompting them to post the following message to Twitter (Twitter, 2020).

2. Fastest growing social media app in the world – over 1 billion active users

TikTok has surpassed over 1 billion active users and more than 2 billion downloads on Google Play and Apple's App Store (Wallaroo, 2020). But this isn't the most fascinating fact about the app. The underlying statistics behind the 1 billion number are far more interesting. TikTok is currently available in 155 countries globally (Apptrace, 2020), and it is popular in more than 135 of those countries. Like the story of Fitz and the Tantrums, TikTok provides you with an opportunity to reach nations and markets you never thought possible. It also boasts the highest engagement rates of any social media app, and 9 out of 10 users return to the app multiple times every day. Furthermore, more than 50% of US users are below 35, and it is unbelievably addictive. There is increasing evidence that its users are growing with the app instead of abandoning it as they grow older. That means TikTok users who start at 16 or 18 do not give up the app when they become 20. (Influencer Marketing-Hub, 2020).

All these facts point to an app that provides an unrivaled pool of the most socially active people to market your products and talents to. This far exceeds anything Facebook, Instagram, or Twitter can offer at the moment. And it's getting better every day. As Lucy Rendler-Kaplan, founder of Arkay Marketing & PR, stated, "Once you begin looking at it from a branding lens, the marketing possibilities are almost endless." She further explains that in *"a world where consumers are more skeptical of ads than ever before, raw, un-overly edited videos of people using your brand in their everyday lives will bring in new users than a commercial-type video."* (Wiltshire, 2019).

3. World-class talents and content

TikTok primarily empowers people to create their own content. The company's stated mission is "to capture and present the world's creativity, knowledge, and precious life moments, directly from the mobile phone. TikTok enables everyone to be a creator, and encourages users to share their passion and creative expression through their videos." (ConsUlt Ease Edutech, 2020).

Perhaps the biggest reason TikTok has become a massive success is because of its premium content. The New York Times TV critic James Poniewozik describes his experience on TikTok as follows:

> *"The scene: someone's backyard. The star: a pine cone, to which someone has attached googly eyes, Popsicle-stick arms, and a string. An unseen force tugs on the line, and the pine cone (his name is Willy) ascends spiraling heavenward, to the gushing chorus of Josh Groban's "You Raise Me Up."*
>
> *The video is 11 seconds of perfect idiocy. I have laughed every time I watched it; I am laughing as I type this out. It's absurd and low-tech and parodic, but also — can an inanimate seed cluster be joyful? Well, this one is. The clip is like the climax to an inspirational movie no one will ever make.*

> This, I discovered after recently downloading TikTok for the first time, is the beauty of the platform. Like Vine before it, it's all climaxes. It's all punch lines and dance outbursts and dramatic (or comedic) reveals." (New York Times, 2019).

Similar experiences have been described time and time again by the countless people who have experienced TikTok. It is an app unlike most other social media apps. According to Oberlo, what makes TikTok "stand out among the competition is that it's more of an entertainment platform, instead of a lifestyle platform. And what makes it so attractive is that practically anyone can become a content provider because of the simplicity of using the app. That's why it appeals to so many content creators around the world." (Oberlo, 2020).

4. Unique Algorithm – optimized to reward creativity

Another very unique feature of TikTok is its special algorithm. Although far from perfect, TikTok's algorithms are most likely to reward your authenticity, creativity, and self-expression. It is also one of the few social media platforms in which previous history does not necessarily play a role in making your posts popular. As TikTok put it, while "a video is likely to receive more views if posted by an account that has more followers, by virtue of that account having built up a larger follower base, neither follower count nor whether the account has had previous high-performing videos are direct factors in the recommendation system" (Wired, 2020). Therefore, theoretically, a person starting out has a good shot at success as one with lots of followers.

When you open the TikTok app on your smartphone, you immediately see the *For You* page. This page features an endless stream of videos uniquely tailored to suit the interests of each user. For TikTok users and creators, the biggest goal is always to be featured in as many *For You* pages as possible. This is the straightest path to going viral. So how exactly does TikTok choose which videos to show each user? TikTok released a Blog post (TikTok, 2020) in June 2020 to explain precisely how it works.

Here are all the essential things you need to know about getting your videos on people's *For You* pages:

a. Sampling: According to Wired, when "a video is uploaded to TikTok, the For You algorithm shows it first to a small subset of users. These people may or may not follow the creator already, but TikTok has determined they may be more likely to engage with the video, based on their past behavior. If they respond favorably—say, by sharing the video or watching it in full—TikTok then shows it to more people who it thinks share similar interests. That same process then repeats itself, and if this positive feedback loop happens enough times, the video can go viral. But if the initial group of guinea pigs don't signal they enjoyed the content, it's shown to fewer users, limiting its potential reach." (Wired, 2020).

b. Watch time and Engagement rate: A very important factor in having your videos shown on lots of *For you* pages is whether people actually watched your video to the end. If people – especially the early subset of users – skip your video after a few seconds, it is unlikely to get recommended to as many people. Therefore, the higher the watch time of your videos, the more people it will be shown to. Also important is the interest people show while watching your video. If they share or comment or like it and follow you, it is likely to create a ripple effect that can make you go viral. Conversely, if users choose *Not Interested* for your videos, or if they choose to hide it, it is unlikely to be shown to too many other people (Houghton, 2019) (Celebrity Access, 2019).

c. Timing: Timing influences TikTok's algorithm, and the time you post your videos can be very important in determining its success. If you post a video while your audience is asleep, it will not do too well. Therefore you can try to plan all your content ahead of time. You can shoot your videos and edit them to an appealing quality before saving them as drafts on TikTok. The drafts can then be posted at the perfect time for getting the most results.

The following are the best times to post on TikTok

Monday	6 am	10 am	10 pm
Tuesday	2 am	4 am	9 am
Wednesday	7 am	8 am	11 pm
Thursday	9 am	12 pm	7 pm
Friday	5 am	1 pm	3 pm
Saturday	11 am	7 pm	8 pm
Sunday	7 am	8 am	4 pm

d. Other factors: Many other factors influence the TikTok algorithm's decision to show videos on the *For You* pages of people. Hashtags, soundtracks or song clips, language preferences, the type of device you use, captions, and country/location (Alexander, 2020) also play some part in featuring videos. Creativity can also play an important role. According to TikTok, some videos may be up to 3 months old when shown on people's feed. Therefore, creativity should always take precedence over speed for every TikTok content creator (McGlew, 2020).

USING TIKTOK FOR YOUR BUSINESS

After explaining all about TIkTok in the above sections, the question running through your mind is probably, how can I use TikTok for my business? And what type of businesses can teenage girls run on TikTok?

Here is a detailed list of the type of businesses you can have on TikTok, and examples of successful people for each one:

1. Entertainment

If you are a young dancer, musician, comedienne, actress, or magician, you should absolutely get on TikTok as quickly as possible to take advantage of the app's 1 billion users to grow your brand/business. TikTok raises new internet celebrities and micro-influencers every single day, and the number of people who have become hugely successful entertainers because of the platform is nearly endless. Chief among them is the 16-year-old dancer, **Charli D'Amelio.**

Charli D'Amelio is currently TikTok's most popular user, with over 92 million followers as of October 2020. Her rise to fame has been nothing short of incredible because she only began to aggressively post her dance videos on TikTik in June 2019. Since then, Charli has modeled for Prada at the Paris Fashion week and accompanied Bebe Rexha to open for the Jonas Brothers at the Barclay Center in Brooklyn. She has just become the face of Hollister alongside her sister, Dixie D'Amelio, and she is currently worth over $4 million according to Forbes (Forbes, 2020).

2. Photography and Videography

Another very good business to bring to TikTok is your photography/videography business. If you're not skilled at photography/videography, you can learn from the many free and paid courses online.

One of the most successful examples on TikTok is **Natalia Seth**. She is a 20-year-old photographer and Photoshop expert. She picked up photography at 12 and began posting her portraits via Instagram. Then she moved to TikTok, which propelled her to become one of the most popular internet influencers. She currently has over 1.9 million TikTok followers, and she's launched her photo book and phone cases, both of which she markets via TikTok.

2. Cosmetics

The wonderful thing about TikTok is that there is an opportunity for most types of businesses that young girls would admire. Yes, you can also promote your makeup and cosmetics business on TikTok. If you already consider yourself excellent at choosing and applying makeup, you might want to consider converting this skill into a business. Alternatively, if you like cosmetics, but you feel you can't really call yourself an expert, you shouldn't be too bothered. There are thousands of courses and YouTube videos to train you every step of the way until you become an expert. Here are a few leading places to get free training/courses:

- **Youtube:** There are so many free cosmetic video tutorials on YouTube, some of which are offered by reputable people/institutions. Just search on Youtube and take your pick.
- **Skillshare:** another portal for great makeup training and tutorials is Skillshare. While not all the courses are free, you can get a free trial when you signup. Here is how to access the makeup/cosmetic courses: https://www.skillshare.com/browse/makeup
- **Formula Botanica:** This is one of the world's leading training institution for cosmetics, and they offer free "Organic & Natural Skincare" training. Here is how you can access the course: https://formulabotanica.com/natural-skincare-training-videos/

There are so many successful cosmetic brands on TikTok. From Kylie Jenner's Kylie Cosmetics to Rihanna's Fenty. However, one of the most amazing stories is that of **Audacity Cosmetics** by 18-year-old Monica Silva. According to her, all "lip care products are made with love, and are 100% vegan and cruelty-free!". Starting with nothing and working alone, with the help of TikTok she now delivers her products worldwide. She has amassed a sizeable social media following with almost 600 thousand followers on TikTok.

4. Fashion

Of course, Fashion brands are making a killing on TikTok. Brands like PrettyLittleThing, Urban Outfitters, Nike, and FashionNova are all doing very well. If you are a young girl with a passion for fashion, TikTok provides an opportunity to outperform even major brands. To put it differently, the traditional playbook for succeeding in Fashion is irrelevant in the age of TikTok. Your ability to create viral videos can place you above some of the world's most iconic brands. Additionally, because of the demographics on TikTok, you can have a reliable customer base for the foreseeable future.

One TikTok user who has been soaring to new heights is 21-year-old Jordyn, with the TikTok account **bydroj**. She is an artist who began making art prints for t-Shirts and tops via TikTok. She now owns an online store that boasts hundreds of thousands of TikTok followers.

5. Jewelry

Selling earrings, necklaces, watches, bracelets, and other jewelry is another excellent business idea that can thrive on TikTok. The great thing about selling jewelry through TikTok is that the niche is not as competitive as singers/dancers. Most big jewelry and watch brands use popular celebrities to promote their products on TikTok. However, one girl who is breaking all the success rules is the TikTok account **@ceo.liv .**

She started her jewelry business at 16, offering customized jewelry, such as designing your name on necklaces and bracelets. Today, she has built a large following with over 1.4 million followers on TikTok, and she has a very successful online store, making sales to all parts of the world.

6. Candles

I bet you didn't think selling candles via TikTok can be an excellent business idea. TikTok user **@taylortoks** also known as CEO of Candles would disagree with you.

Taylortoks She posts instructional videos such as "how to light a candle properly" and "how to upgrade your patio in 30 minutes." She has built a considerable following on TikTok with over 1.3 million likes and 24.5 thousand followers. She makes beautiful and nicely scented candles, and she has sold thousands of products by promoting on TikTok.

7. Cakes

You can also design cakes and promote them on TikTok. A very successful example is Allie Meadows, with the TikTok account **@allie_meadows**.

Allie_meadows She is a 16-year-old self-taught baker from Nashville, Tennessee, and she constantly posts videos showing how she makes all her cakes. She has gone viral because of this, and she has since made it possible to order cakes through a small website and direct messages. Additionally, she has a GoFundMe page, making it possible for people worldwide to support her business. As of August 2020, Allie had about 228 thousand TikTok followers.

The list of businesses that can be promoted on TikTok is limitless. Further examples like cooking, fitness training, yoga, driving, sports, teaching, taking care of pets, personal hygiene, activism, motivation, and counseling, among others, can also easily go viral on the app. Whatever you are good at doing, or whatever you feel you might be interested in doing, become better at it and start creatively promoting yourself on TikTok.

THE 3 MAIN WAYS YOU CAN USE TIKTOK AS A BUSINESS

There are three main ways to use TikTok as a business. First is through ads, second is to grow your account organically, and finally, you can also use micro-influencers. Each of these will be discussed extensively in subsequent chapters; however, here is a brief explanation of the three:

1. **Running ads:** Without running ads, it might be challenging to scale your business significantly. This is because TikTok initially only shows your posts to people from the same country as your mobile number. However, ads would cost you some money, and it might not be so easy when starting with nothing.

2. **Growing organically:** You can grow your business/brand organically on TikTok by constantly posting creative videos and participating in challenges and Hashtags. If your videos are brilliant enough, you might go viral, which would provide a springboard for your business.

3. **Using micro-influencers:** Micro-influencers are TikTok users with between 5 thousand to 10 thousand followers. You can partner with them to promote your products, and it costs between $20 - $50 for each post. They are much cheaper than full influencers, but if you are smart about it, they can have as much impact for your business.

CHAPTER TWO: CREATING A PERFECT TIKTOK PROFILE

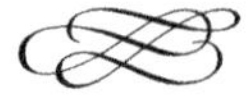

"Too late, I found you can't wait to become perfect, you got to go out and fall down and get up with everybody else."

— **RAY BRADBURY**

How can you begin your TikTok journey and create an enchanting profile?

It is straightforward to create an account on TikTok. It is also easy to create multiple accounts if you intend to separate your personal profile from your business. You only need to follow a few rules for this. You must keep in mind that you cannot create an additional account using the same information linked to your existing account. For example, two accounts cannot share the same phone number or email address.

Here is a step-by-step guide for creating your TikTok profile:

WHAT YOU NEED TO CREATE A NEW TIKTOK PROFILE

To create a TikTok account, you'll need the following:

1. Phone number, email address, Apple id or other social media accounts like Instagram, Twitter and Facebook: you can only create an account by using one of the above methods.

2. A smartphone: TikTok is a mobile app, and although you can log in via your PC, it functions primarily for mobile devices.

3. The TikTok app: to create a TikTok account, you must download the app from either Apple's App Store or Google Play.

4. Internet connection: It seems basic, but you'll need an internet connection to use the app.

5. Username: To create a TikTok account, you'll be asked to choose a username. It is important to choose a username that is perfect for your business.

HOW TO CREATE A NEW TIKTOK ACCOUNT

1. Download the TikTok app from Apple's App Store or Google Play.

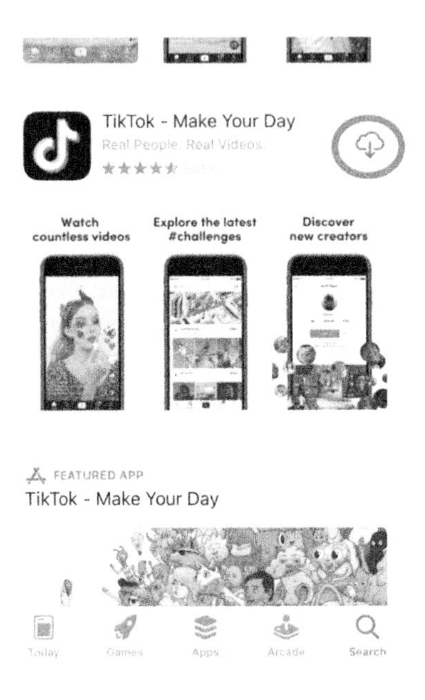

2. Open the app, and you will immediately be asked to **"Sign up for TikTok."**

3. You can create a new account in several ways. The easiest is to use your phone number. To use your phone number, Tap on "Use phone or email" among the several options on your screen.

4. Next, you will be asked to enter your birthday. Don't worry; it won't be shown publicly.

5. After entering your date of birth, you'll be asked to enter

your phone number or email. To use your phone number, tap on **"Phone."** And enter your phone number.

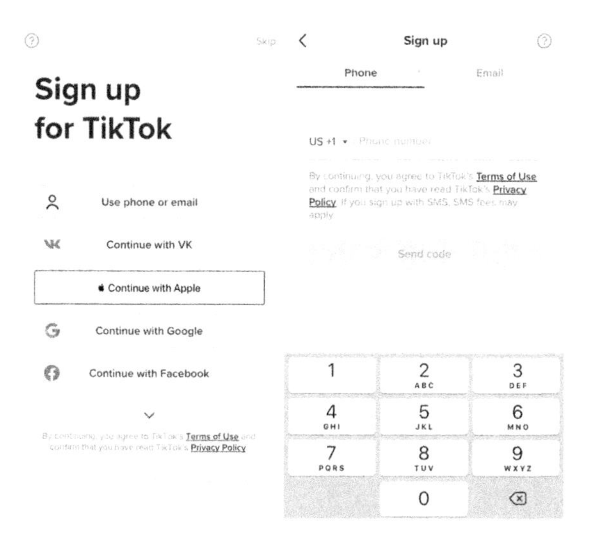

6. Click on send code after entering your number. You will automatically receive an SMS with a 4-digit code.

7. Enter the code on the app and your account would be created.

8. Next you will be asked to create your **username.**

9. If you prefer to use email, from Step 5, tap **"email"** instead of phone. Then, enter your email and click on **next.**

10. Enter your password and click on **next.**

11. Then select a username and tap on **"register"** to create your new account.

ADDING A NEW ACCOUNT TO AN EXISTING TIKTOK PROFILE

If you already have a TikTok account, but you are thinking of making a different one for your business, or starting afresh, here is how you can create a new account from an existing profile:

HOW TO CREATE A NEW ACCOUNT ON TIKTOK USING YOUR PHONE NUMBER

1. Open the TikTok application on your iPhone or Android.
2. Tap on **"Me"** and then on your username.
3. Tap on **"Add account."**
4. Tap **"Use phone or email."**
5. Enter your date of birth.
6. Enter your phone number to receive a 4-digit code and to complete the account creation process.

HOW TO CREATE A NEW ACCOUNT ON TIKTOK USING YOUR EMAIL ADDRESS

1. Open the TikTok app on your phone.

2. Tap on **"Me"** and then on your username.

4. Tap **"Add account."**

5. Tap **"Use phone or email."**

6. Enter your date of birth.

7. Tap on **"Email"** at the top.

8. Enter your email address, then tap on **"Next."**

9. You will be asked to choose a password and a username to complete the account creation process.

HOW TO CREATE A NEW ACCOUNT ON TIKTOK USING A SOCIAL NETWORK ACCOUNT

1. Open the TikTok application.

2. Tap on **"Me,"** then on your username and on **"Add account."**

5. TikTok accepts most popular social media accounts, including your Google, Twitter, Instagram, or Facebook accounts.

P.S. *For iPhone users, a pop-up message may warn you that "TikTok" wants to use" X.com "to connect," "X" being the name of the social networking service you have chosen. Tap on* ***"Continue."***

6. Enter your login information for the social media you have chosen.

7. Finally, you'll be asked to select a username to complete the process.

HOW TO NAVIGATE TIKTOK

After creating your TikTok account, you will be immediately brought to TikTok's main page, featuring videos "For You" and a lot of functions.

1. **Home:** This is the main page of TikTok. It shows you streams of videos tailored to meet your interests, based on your followers, watch history, location, and other factors.

2. **Discover:** You use this function to search for people, videos, songs, hashtags, or challenges. It also features the trending videos and hashtags on TikTok.

3. **Plus (+):** You use this function to take/upload videos to TikTok by simply tapping on it.

4. **Inbox:** This function enables you to chat with other TikTok users and creators via direct messaging.

5. **Me:** This is the 'settings' function of TikTok. It helps you to do everything from changing your name to adding a bio, profile picture, or social media account, among others. It also shows you your upload history and the performance of your previous videos.

HOW TO ENGAGE WITH TIKTOK VIDEOS

If you watch a TikTok video you like, you might be interested in leaving a comment, liking the video, or sharing it with your friends on other social media or messaging apps.

All the functions are located on the right side of the video. To like a video, tap on the heart symbol, and to leave a comment, tap on the speech symbol. You can also share the video using the forward or WhatsApp sign, depending on if you've added other social media accounts to your TikTok.

CHOOSING A PERFECT USERNAME FOR TIKTOK

What is a TikTok username?

A username is a personal identifier that can make you stand out on TikTok and other social media platforms. It must be different from any other account, and it can be a powerful branding tool for a person or business. TikTok allows any combination of letters, numbers, and symbols for usernames.

Why is it important to have a good username?

Selecting a good username can make or break your TikTok account. There are a lot of reasons why having a good username is important on TikTok. The most important reason is that usernames are indexed by the search algorithm, which provides an opportunity for you to use it to your advantage. Contrary to popular belief, if you're starting out on TikTok today intending to create your business, it makes more sense to use your business name or niche as part of your username and not your actual name. Examples can be: adelecakes or natalie_dancer, for example. This is reasonable because you will already be entering your name into a different section on TikTok, and it's a waste of an opportunity to enter your full name twice. Instead, you can enter your real name into the name category and your business name or idea into the username section.

Furthermore, usernames must also be unique, and they can be changed once every 30 days, allowing you to make corrections to a name you don't like.

Rules to follow when choosing a username

1. Remember, it is an opportunity to boost your profiles on search algorithms.
2. Your username should say something about you.
3. It should be the name of your company or brand.

4. Keep it simple, short, and memorable.
5. Don't use too many special characters, because people can't remember them. Avoid names like **@so__na__123**.
6. Don't use several letters in a row, like **@ana.souzaaaaa**.
7. Don't add a random string of numbers at the end, like **@football333333**.
8. It is an opportunity to make an impression on people.
9. Avoid controversial or offensive words or names.

Tips for obtaining your dream username if someone already has your name

1. Add "I am" before your name, for example **@imcesarmillan**
2. Add an adjective to your name. For example, **greatcardi, awesome.ann, expert.charlie, etc.**
3. Add the name of your industry, for example **@boschpowertools.**
4. Combine your name with your product or industry, for example **@lucydancer** and **@allieartist.**
5. Add ".com" to your name if you have a website, for example **@lovehockey.com**
6. Add "TikTok" to your username, for example **@tiktokhoopers**.
7. Add your location if you have a physical store, for example **@mcdonaldsfrance**.
8. Add "official" at the end, for example **@nickiofficial**.
9. Add other words that help your business **@getflexseal**, **@staytunednbc**.

Finally, if you're a popular brand and you find accounts that have your name and pretend to be you, you can report them to TikTok, and they'll take them down.

WRITING YOUR TIKTOK BIO

It is difficult for many people to describe everything about them or their businesses concisely, so the bio section is especially challenging for them. On TikTok, the bio is limited to 80 characters, so users need to be incredibly savvy in maximizing this section's potential.

Why is your bio important?

LIKE MEETING someone for the first time, your bio is one of the first things people see about you online. It should tell them about who you are or what you do, or about your personality. It should do all these things without being boring or confusing.

You can do the following before writing your bio:

- Look at people in your industry for inspiration.
- Identify your Business Personality.
- Keep your target group or audience in mind.
- What you want people to know about your product.

Types of bio you can write

There are three main types of bio you can write for TikTok. We have the list bio, the 1-2 sentences bio, and the hook bio. Here is an explanation of the three types, featuring examples from successful TikTok users:

1. List Bio: this type of bio lists short things that describe you or your business. It is a compelling type of bio because it uses a bulleting system to succinctly describe your products or brand. Gary Vaynerchuk, with tiktok username @garyvee is a perfect example of this. Here is how he does it below:

2. 1-2 sentence bio: this involves using one or two sentences to describe yourself or your business/brand. This is a very popular system on many leading TikTok accounts. Some excellent examples are the accounts of @extremeofficial, @nfl, @imcesarmillan. Here is how they do it below:

@extremeofficial does it in one simple, direct and explanatory sentence.

@nfl adds some humor, while staying on message. They also use one concise sentence.

@imcesarmillan uses two short sentences, including a pitch for a product, in this case, his YouTube channel.

3. Hook bio: the final type of bio is the hook bio. This involves giving people a reason to follow you or buy your product by offering something to them in return, like a follow back, or a free product. Kylie Cosmetics does this by asking people to participate in a challenge in exchange for cosmetics.

USING EMOJIS ON YOUR TIKTOK BIO

An effortless way to direct people's attention to your link is to use an arrow or hand emoji. Furthermore, a brilliant way to make your bio stand out is to add lively and captivating emojis to it. From the above examples, @extremeofficial and @garyvee are two profiles that use emojis to make their bio more engaging. However, they are not alone at this. Some of the biggest stars in the world use emojis on their bio.

Here are a few examples:

ADDING LINKS TO YOUR TIKTOK BIO

TikTok makes it possible to add links to your bio. If you are a business or brand, you might want to add links to your online store or your YouTube/Soundcloud/Spotify channel if you're a musician or entertainer. You might also simply be interested in adding links to your other social media accounts such as your Instagram or Twitter to build your followership across all platforms. Furthermore, you can add links to GoFundMe or Patreon – or other donation websites – to receive donations to your business or cause. Whatever the reason, there are a few things to know before adding links to your account. The first of which is that there are 2 types of links you can add to your TikTok account. I explain them extensively below:

1. Pinned links

These types of links are perfect for your other social media accounts, like Instagram and YouTube. They also make it very easy to automatically share your TikTok videos on your other social media accounts without needing to save and upload every time.

2. Regular links in bio

Regular links are a way to add your business website or online store to your TikTok account. TikTok recently added a feature to place clickable web links on your profile. To do this, follow the steps below:

How to add Instagram, YouTube, and website to TikTok

Step 1: Open your TikTok app and tap the **"Me"** or profile icon at the bottom-right corner of your screen.

Step 2: Tap on "Edit Profile."

Step 3: Scroll down to **"Websites"** and enter your weblink.

Step 4: Scroll down and tap on "Add Instagram" if you want to add your Instagram account and/or "Add YouTube" if you wish to add your YouTube.

Step 5: For Instagram, you will be prompted to enter your Instagram username and password. Enter your details and tap "Log In."

Step 6: If you use an iPhone, you will be asked to "Authorize"

TikTok to enable the app to access your Instagram information. Tap on "Authorize."

Step 7: Your Instagram account will be added automatically. The process is similar for YouTube.

USING LINKTREE TO ADD MULTIPLE LINKS TO TIKTOK

There are many reasons why people might want to add more than one link to their website section on TikTok. If you are a singer, you might want to add links to your personal website and links to your songs/music videos. If your business is in a different industry, you might want to add a link to your online shops. The most popular way to do this is to use **Linktree – linktr.ee**.

Linktree is a free landing page for hosting multiple links to social media and websites. It is used by many popular brands and celebrities. A big example is Bebe Rexha. You can find a photo of her TikTok page in the previous section, with a visible Linktree link in place of her website. Here is exactly how her Linktree page looks like:

CREATING A PERFECT PROFILE PICTURE FOR TIKTOK

There are a few things to keep in mind when deciding on your profile picture for TikTok. First, you must remember that, similar to Instagram, your followers cannot expand your profile picture. Therefore, you must go with something stunning. Something that can captures the attention of your audience while staying true to yourself. Your profile picture must be easily recognizable to any user despite the small space it occupies.

If you are starting out as a business, you might add a picture perfectly depicting what you offer, or you might instead opt for your brand's logo. Take a look at Nike's TikTok profile picture below:

HOW CAN YOU DESIGN AN INEXPENSIVE BUT EXCELLENT LOGO FOR TIKTOK?

Making a fabulous logo doesn't have to be expensive. Just take the example above. The Nike logo and brand is perhaps the most reputable in the world. It is so extraordinary that Steve Jobs famously aspired to make Apple's marketing and brand on par with it. How much did Nike pay to design its logo? Only $35. Nike's co-founder Phil Knight commissioned graphic design student Carolyn Davidson to create the Nike swoosh logo for $35 in 1971.

You can make an excellent logo for less than the $35 Nike paid for its logo in the current age. Here is how to do it.

Design a logo with free online tools

You can design a logo without paying a penny using one of the many free logo creation tools on the internet. While many of those tools/websites aren't worth your time, a few of them offer very outstanding results. Here are two examples:

1. **Wix's Logo Maker:** Wix.com is one of the world's leading web development companies. It also provides a free logo creator on its website, which can help you create a brand logo in minutes. All you need to do is answer a few questions about your business and personal style, and the tool will create a logo for you. It also makes it possible to edit the logo until it perfectly suits your taste. You can access Wix's logo maker here: https://www.wix.com/logo/maker

2. **Logomaster.ai:** This is another world-class web tool that helps you to create a logo within a few minutes. You will also be asked to enter your business name and add a few details about your business. They do not charge any fees for designing your logo, but you will be asked to pay some fee before saving it, which is only after you are satisfied with the results. You can access the Logomaster.ai logo creator here: https://logomaster.ai/

Hire a Freelance graphic designer

You can hire a freelance graphic designer from websites like **Fiverr** (fiverr.com) or **Upwork** (upwork.com) or **99 designs** (99designs.com). You can hire an expert designer for as low as $20, and all 3 websites offer clients the opportunity to make revisions to orders if you are not satisfied with the outcome.

Before selecting a graphic designer on the above websites, there are a few things to note to help you find brilliant designers.

1. **Read the reviews:** Only offer your job to a designer with sterling reviews from previous customers. This tells you that the person has the requisite experience and talent to provide a good service.

2. **Check the earned history:** Make sure your designer has earned at least $500 from previous jobs on the websites. This is just as important as the first requirement. It tells you the person is a genuine freelancer.

3. **Fully communicate exactly what you want:** Provide every tiny piece of relevant information for the job. For freelancers, information is never too much. Let them know exactly what you want and how you want it. This will help you avoid wasting time with numerous revisions.

4. **Make sure your designer provides revisions:** Because logos can sometimes be very personal, make sure any designer you hire provides an opportunity to make unlimited revisions. You can discuss this ahead of time.

5. **Ask for different file formats:** Make sure your designer agrees to provide you with high-resolution images in several file formats such as JPG and PSD. This will save you trouble in the future if you need different versions of your logo.

6. **Get all the rights to your logo:** Most freelancers usually transfer all rights upon completing a job, but it's not a bad idea to confirm this before hiring a freelancer.

7. **Hire more than one:** It is always better to hire 4 people

than to hire one. That way, you can assign the best person to each task of the project.

8. Interview the selected freelancers: Almost all popular freelance websites provide a method to interview freelancers. Talk to your potential freelancers before deciding on the perfect candidates.

9. Look to Eastern Europe and Southeast Asia for talent: Unlike writing, graphic design doesn't require fluency in a specific language. Therefore, you should consider hiring freelancers from Eastern Europe or Southeast Asia because many of them are talented and cheaper.

CHAPTER THREE: HOW TO MAKE GREAT VIDEOS ON TIKTOK

"You can tell how much viewers enjoy your videos by how long they watch"

— **NICK NIMMIN**

As has been repeated throughout this book, videos are everything on TikTok. Videos are the primary way you can make posts and go viral on the app. For an aspiring TikTok business person, the importance of getting your videos right cannot be overemphasized.

TikTok rules stipulate that your videos should not exceed a maximum of 60 seconds, leaving you with less than 15 seconds to make an instant impression on your viewers. There are different types of videos you can create. Here are some of the biggest ones:

There are 3 significant types of TikTok videos:

- **Recreation videos**: These are enjoyable videos intended to relax, entertain, and pass an important message at the same time. For example, someone using TikTok frequently might run across numerous dance videos. Creators use it to demonstrate their dance skills and call on other people to engage in a dance challenge. If you have a talent for dancing or comedy, this video type will certainly help market your skills.

- **Reaction Videos**: Reaction videos show people's responses to various events or another person's post. For example, if you post a video responding to the unrest surrounding police brutality, you're posting a reaction video.
- **Relatable Videos:** These videos demonstrate a causal or logical connection to something. Examples of relatable videos are videos about life under quarantine, videos about having trouble with a spouse, or videos about the troubles of the year 2020 (Financial Times, 2019).

IDEAS FOR NEW TIKTOK VIDEOS

Thriving on TikTok requires that you frequently upload interesting content. This can be sometimes difficult to achieve but without the right ideas.

Here are some ideas for you to consider:

Tutorial Videos

All types of tutorials perform well on TikTok. People are open to discovering new things, especially when they can learn in less than 60 seconds. TikTok is popular with quick-cooking tutorials and how to dance tutorials, and how to use cosmetics tutorials. There are even tutorials about how to light and open a bottle properly, among others.

Fitness is another trending topic on TikTok with plenty of tips and perspectives from instructors on achieving your weight goals. Whatever business you are engaged in, find a way to make it more enjoyable with a tutorial: fashion tips, product samples, or others. There are endless possibilities.

Here are some tutorial videos dominating TikTok:

- **The "Kill This Love" Dance:** When they released the single "Kill This Love" in 2019, the band Blackpink dominated the music world, and the choreography of the music video inspired hundreds of TikTok users. Some of the most famous TikTok videos of 2019 were dance videos to the "Kill This Love" soundtrack (Martinez, 2019).

And who can give a lesson on the dance better than the Blackpink group themselves? They created a practice video demonstrating how to perfect the moves. A step-by-step guide is also available for those who need a little more guidance.

- **How to use Bronzer and Contour Correctly:** There are even more ingenious makeover tutorials on TikTok than dance challenges and memes. Beauty experts and influencers are on the platform in large groups and teach all the latest tricks and tips.

Makeup artist @makeupbymaritsa states that indeed, the contouring powder and bronzer are different. She also illustrates how to apply them to appear as if you have been trained in professional makeup.

- **Cooking with Shereen (@cookingwithshereen)**

Do you know your amazing aunt, who always comes with the best dishes at family gatherings? Chef Shereen's going to remind you of her. Whether it's a home-made pasta, noodle soup, Sunday sauce, a more unusual thing, like lobster mac 'n' cheese, she's got your back. Her tutorials are warm, welcoming, and excellent ways of breaking down the fundamentals of many dishes (TikTok, 2020)

Behind-the-Scenes Videos

Behind the scenes, videos are an ideal way to make the business and staff more likable. Emphasize everyday tasks, workplaces, development processes, and more. Interview personnel, speak to your suppliers, or talk to your best customers. Each of these things helps the viewer understand the way your business operates and reveals your identity. Such videos promote brand identity and help build trust. As followers connect with online brands, they sometimes cannot feel the brand's presence strongly. The brand personality can be hard to express on a screen with just a few characters. Tutorial videos provide the possibility to dig into something remarkable about a company. The relationship between company and customer will develop with a fantastic video behind the scenes, and if the video is entertaining or insightful, it will become viral.

You could opt for a tutorial video if you are a chef or have a cake-making business; a behind the scenes video showing your food being cooked or your cake being prepared. This can be useful for almost any type of business. For a dancer, a behind the scenes video can show you practicing – and failing – to learn a new move.

Here are some examples of some ideas for behind the scenes videos on TikTok:

- **What It's Like to Work for You**

Going behind the scenes is a great way to explain your experience to prospective clients. Add your own video footage and images to show you what it's like to work with you.

- **Explain How the Product Is Produced**

Showcase what's exclusive about your brand. Showing how the product is made will make your customers prefer it over similar companies. A video like this helps you not only to view the product but also to express your personality and beliefs. Here's @ceo.liv showing how she makes her jewelry.

- **Take Viewers on a Virtual Tour**

Display your workspace with the Behind-the-Scenes video. Notably, a video like this will help people know what to expect before their first appointment, especially if you meet your clients in person.

Videos Answering Customer Questions (Live QA Sessions)

Interview videos are the ideal way to create brand credibility, and they offer the viewers an immersive experience about your brand and personality. They typically involve answering questions from people about your product, brand, or other topics.

It is also an excellent way to create long term bonding experiences with your audience. Another interview strategy is to create a series of videos with guests/influencers, using their expertise to boost your content marketing. The more you do this, the more reputation you earn from the interaction with brands. The people you interview can also share the videos via their channels, making your videos even more popular.

Here are some steps to ensure that your question and answer works well:

- **Engagement:** Don't lose sight of what matters most during your live stream – your dedication and viewer engagement. It would be best to concentrate on keeping your viewers interested during a question & answer session. You may also take advantage of the opportunity to ask questions and learn more about them.

- **Promotion:** A question and answer session would not work without an audience. To ensure your audience joins your broadcast, it is crucial to promote your live video as much as possible.
- **Call-to-Action:** Don't forget why you do a live question and answer. If you are promoting a product, an eBook, or want users to subscribe to your channel, include a specific call-to-action to drive your viewers to your target.

Testimonial videos

Presentations and customer reviews are excellent video content, but testimonials are another smart way to take things to a new level. By focusing on an existing client, you can prove that your brand – and the goods and services it provides – make customers happy. The important thing here is to use genuine customers. Do not recruit actors! Contact your satisfied client-base instead, and ask them to come up with an honest video testimonial. This can incentivize them to post testimonials on their social media and send them to you... For example, you could promise gifts or a discount on their next purchase to anyone who records a video testimonial for you.

Here are some rules for successful testimonials on TikTok:

- **Don't overwhelm the viewer:** It is a good idea to appeal to audiences' feelings while catering to their rational side. Don't overwhelm them with a lot of details. Instead, the person making your testimonial should mention one or two impressive reasons why they love your product or brand.

- **Add visual effects:** Adding visual appeal to your video testimonials is a fantastic way to catch viewers' attention. You can also highlight the advantages of your brand in the description. Moreover, on the screen, don't post only text. Try to add visual effects. They animate the testimonials and make them more appealing. You can also use various font settings, add small illustrations, and employ other techniques. If you have to outsource it to get a perfect quality, use Upwork. You will love the results.

THE MOST VITAL ELEMENTS FOR AN EFFECTIVE POST

TikTok is primarily a video sharing platform; however, many elements accompany every video upload. To create a compelling post, you must add a few details like video titles, descriptions, and hashtags.

You can first record your video by clicking on the plus (+) button on the app's screen. It will automatically use your phone's front-facing. It also provides a lot of features that can help you to edit as you create.

TITLES AND TEXT

The algorithm of TikTok lets favorite videos appear in more feeds as shares and likes build up. This helps posts gain trending status in a short time. It does not discriminate or concentrate on a small group of users. A crucial part of achieving success is getting your titles right. Titles are often overlooked, but they play a key role in keeping people viewing your videos longer, which can boost you on TikTok's algorithm. They are a great way to add value to your video, and they can also be a good substitute for your voice by explaining your video via text. Moreover, titles can also help your videos go viral in countries where people don't speak English very well.

A good title is accurate, light-hearted, and entertaining. There is a particular skill in choosing titles. People have very short attention spans, and your video's title will be one of the first items that they look at when deciding whether to invest their valuable time in your video or not.

How to add TITLES and TEXT to a video

After recording your video content, you can review it and edit as much as you'd like before finally posting it. Under review, click on the "Text" icon at the bottom of the screen. If you want the text to show up at a specific time in the video, click on "Set duration." You can also select the color of the text or the background you want from the colored bubbles above your phone's keyboard. You can even change the font to any of the many available on TikTok.

When adding text, keep in mind that if you put it too close to the bottom or the side, it will be covered by other elements like your description, hashtags, or profile picture.

SOUNDS/SONGS

The site consists of short clips that are not editable. There are no complete songs on TikTok. In other words, you may be out of luck if you dream of making flosses to a specific part of your favorite album. But this dilemma can be solved. Many TikTok users play a song from another device, such as a laptop or a stereo. TikTok can record the track as an "Original clip," which can be added to other users' videos. However, this loophole can lead to copyright violations.

Alternatively, you can simply use sound clips from the millions of authorized songs on TikTok. This way, you avoid breaking any copyright rules and choose from the list of trending songs that can make your videos go viral.

Why is it Important to Use Songs?

There is a better chance for songs to go viral, particularly in non-English speaking countries. Music is sometimes a more powerful emotional connector than words. The songs can sway an individual's emotional state, convincing them to buy the advertised product without immediate resistance. It also has another obvious benefit. The music draws in the audience and captures their attention. Songs can comfortably fit into a standard time of 60 seconds for a TikTok video.

3 Ways to Use Sounds

- **Free TikTok Sounds**: To add TikTok sounds, open the camera and click on 'sounds' on top of the screen before you hit record. This will open a music menu, which will allow you to either choose a famous clip, a song, or a sound from the search bar.
- **Use Your Voice Recordings**: The use of your voice

recordings brings individuality to your brand. You become likable to your audience because they can relate to you on a personal level.

- **Brand Creators**: You can also use voice-overs from famous actors, such as those seen on TVs, movies, or Youtube. Although this may cause you to dig deeper into your wallet, it will eventually make your brand more successful with TikTok.

How to Add Sound to a Video

Music is central to TikTok. One of the reasons a video might go viral could be that it plays a famous song. Here is how one can add songs.

Step 1: Click Add Sound to the left of the recording screen.

Step 2: The streaming menu of artists and records is displayed.

Step 3: Browse to find the most popular tracks and click on the one you want to add to your video.

Step 4: Save your favorite selections by clicking the icon to the right of the song's name.

EFFECTS

TikTok provides a range of editing options, including adding text, changing screen colors, and adding filters and effects, among others. The most effective way of making your TikTok video far more attractive is to add special effects.

How to Use Effects on TikTok Posts

The effects are where the magic happens on TikTok. They simplify creativity and help produce excellent content. Would you like to create videos using effects, such as a green screen?

Step 1: Tap the effects icon on the red record icon's lefthand side to select an effect.

Step 2: Tap on one of the effects to apply it to your video.

Step 3: You can add the effect to your favorites from the Effects tab.

DESCRIPTION AND HASHTAGS

Descriptions are what explain what your post is about. If you're a business person, TikTok users might wish to learn a bit about your business when they see your post. TikTok allows you to personalize the post using description, and you should take the opportunity to make your business more attractive and personal.

TikTok only allows 100 characters for the description, where you can add any additional information you didn't mention in your video. For example, you can ask other users to provide feedback or ideas about your products. This also helps to drive up your engagement stats.

A business person who is starting out should use a mix of popular hashtags, like those with millions of views, and those with fewer views, in the tens of thousands. This makes it possible to take advantage of the best of both worlds without facing too much competition. Remember to use hashtags that are relevant to your content. You can use the following website to help you find relevant hashtags: TikTokHashtags.com.

Don't forget to create your own hashtag to take your TikTok marketing to the next level. It can help you stand out from the crowd and provide you with an opportunity to source user-generated content (Influencer Marketing Hub, 2020)

Hashtags can also function like a phrase, title, or sentence that contributes to sending a strong message. Essentially, hashtags will categorize your posts more effectively. They help you meet the target audience and, above all, help your target audience find you. These users are more likely to engage with your post because it is what they expected. Hashtags are like sales funnels. General marketing is unbelievably vast and caters to all sorts of posts. A more specialized and targeted post can narrow people's search to get what they want; hence you will find the right audience.

How to add descriptions and hashtags to a video

After taking and editing your video, click "Next" to get to the page for adding descriptions and hashtags. Your description needs to contain keywords that direct your target audience to your videos. You can tag friends by writing the person's TikTok account name or adding hashtags in your description.

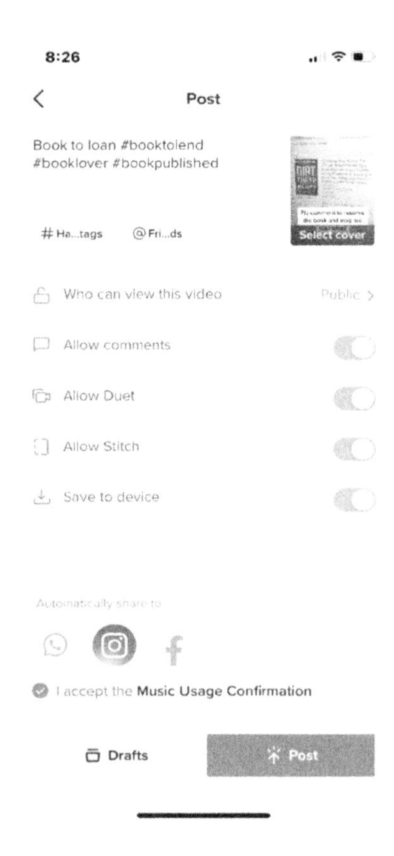

SEE WHAT YOUR COMPETITORS ARE USING

Another way to look for hashtags, effects, and songs is to study the ones used by your competitors. Chances are they might be using what you need to be using. Always keep an eye on what your competitors are doing, but don't rely on that as your primary strategy (Influencer Marketing Hub, 2020).

SEE WHAT'S POPULAR ON THE 'FOR YOU' PAGE

TikTok's 'For You' page is a treasure trove for finding the songs, effects, and hashtags that are popular. If you see 3 videos using a particular style on your 'For You' page, it will probably trend soon, and it's imperative to save it as a favorite by pressing on the video then clicking Save video. Also, follow creators who have already achieved your next goal so you can adopt their methods (StayHipp, 2020) (Paul, 2020).

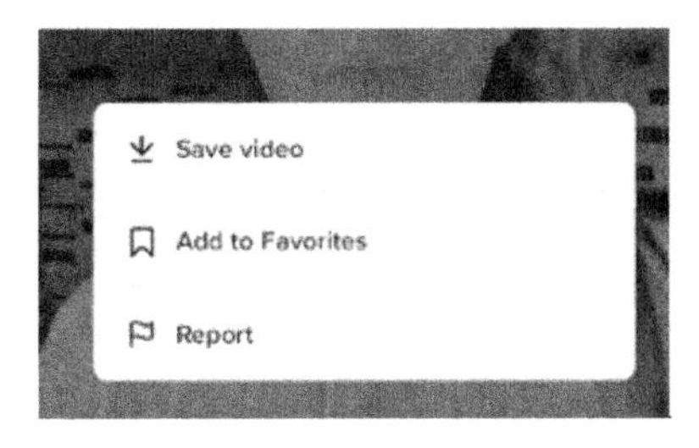

DISADVANTAGES OF RECORDING A VIDEO USING THE TIKTOK APP

The TikTok app offers its own video recording feature with your phone's camera. This feature is not as versatile as videos directly recorded on your phone's camera or an external camera. Videos recorded on TikTok might come with some disadvantages because:

- There is limited functionality for editing.
- The videos carry the TikTok watermark when saved.

HOW TO IMPORT A PRERECORDED VIDEO TO TIKTOK

You might wish to use some videos or pictures in your gallery rather than record directly on the app. TikTok allows you to upload both images and videos. The upload feature is right in the app's video recorder feature. You can upload your prerecorded image by doing the following:

1. Click on the plus (+) icon at the bottom of your screen on the TikTok app. While on the camera screen, click on "Upload" right beside the record button (big red button).

2. The videos and photos on your device will appear when you slide left. Alternatively, you can simply tap on "Image." Select the images, videos, or a combination of both that you wish to use on your TikTok post and then tap on "Next."

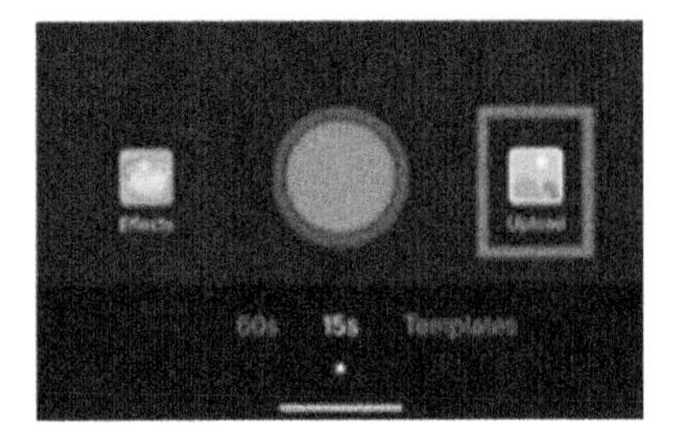

3. Select all the necessary settings to put together your content

and click on "Next." On the following screen, add effects or texts, and after click "Next" to input your desired description, tags, and hashtags. Then click "Next" once more to upload your video.

HOW TO IMPROVE THE QUALITY OF YOUR TIKTOK VIDEOS

Almost every video on TikTok goes through some form of editing. The very best content has been edited to look more appealing and attract many likes, comments, and shares. It is vital to prepare a post ahead of time. That includes preparation for taking the video, editing the video, and adding any captions/descriptions you need to make the video reach a wider audience. Editing a video does not have to be very complicated. It might be as simple as enhancing your videos' quality or adding filters or special effects. Or it might involve cropping out the part of the video you don't like. It can also involve advanced video corrections, using any of the many video editing tools available.

Editing your videos certainly makes them better and can attract a bigger audience to view them. It is especially necessary on TikTok because you have a split second to impress your viewers and capture their attention. The first two seconds of your video is critical. They can be the difference between people scrolling past it or stopping to watch it until the end. Furthermore, people on TikTok do not have the longest attention span, and you are competing with some of the most creative people in the world.

To do significant editing to your videos, you can either use one of the many mobile video editing apps available on Apple's App Store and Google Play. However, the best video editing tools usually require paying a subscription fee.

The easiest way to edit your TikTok videos is to film them using the TikTok app because most people have observed that they get the best results taking videos through TikTok. While recording video content, always remember to make it as short as possible. Many of the most successful videos on TikTok are short, typically in the range of 12 seconds. You don't need any sophisticated production skills to thrive on TikTok. Your creativity is more important for success.

Here are four things to improve the quality of your TikTok videos:

1. Camera: This is the primary way to get better videos. Using better videography hardware is a major part of taking videos. You could get a better phone with a better video/camera quality to enhance your videos' quality. Some of the more recent iPhones and Samsung – among others – have made tremendous upgrades in the camera hardware and software department, making it possible to take 4K high definition (HD) videos. Another way to get a very high-quality video is to buy a professional digital camera. Some of the latest models offer mirrorless cameras that are excellent for both photography and videography. Although they are more expensive, they are much more practical for larger brands with bigger budgets. If you are starting out, you can begin with your phone's camera and strive to buy a professional video camera after scaling your business.

2. Lighting: This is a much-underestimated part of taking quality videos. The lighting contributes considerably to their beauty. For most people starting out, the most common source of lighting is *natural light*. This means the light from the sun that enters your room. If you use natural lighting, make sure you face a window every time you take a video. Ensure the window is not behind you because the light reflection into the camera will almost certainly guarantee poor video quality.

- Popular TikTok content creators use *ring lights* to provide additional lighting for their videos. Ring light significantly improves the quality of the video, and they are very affordable. They cost about $40 and are compatible with iPhones and Androids. Many ring lights also come with stands – a tripod – for holding up both the ring lights and your phone.
- A more expensive setup would be to use *studio lights*. This involves using controlled lighting equipment that is not as affordable as a ring light. Studio lights include high-powered LED lamps, diffusers, reflectors, and soft-boxes, among others. They are too expensive for many TikTok videos, but they can significantly transform the quality of your videos. They are the best option for very big brands or a professional setting.

3. Camera stabilization: Have you ever noticed blurs or uncontrolled movements in videos? This sometimes happens when a person holds their phone while taking a video. It can be difficult to hold your hand still for a long time, more so on TikTok because most videos involve dancing or movements. A smart way around this is to use a tripod. Tripods vary in design. There are tripods with extendable legs, short table tripods, flexible tripods, and even Gimbal stabilizers. They are not too expensive, depending on which type you decide to buy. The prices range from about $15 to about $500. The more expensive ones are usually professional Gimbal stabilizers. The point is to reduce the blur in your videos and minimize your editing time.

4. Microphone: As much as your video's visual elements are important, the audio is just as essential. Although TikTok was initially designed as a lip-syncing platform, it can now be used for video without prerecorded audio. While phones and digital cameras can adequately record audio and videos, you may decide to use an enhancement gadget to boost your audio quality. This might be more crucial for people who intend to sing or talk a lot on their TikTok videos. External microphones independently capture audio better and more clearly than most smartphones. There are different types of mini-shotgun mics for phones and shotgun mics for professionals.

CHAPTER FOUR: HOW TO GROW YOUR ACCOUNT

"What you stay focused on will grow."

— **ROY T. BENNETT**

GROWING YOUR TIKTOK ACCOUNT MEANS INCREASING YOUR number of followers, views, and post engagement to build your business empire. It is the dream of every TikTok user. As explained in previous chapters, TikTok rewards creativity above any other metric. This is a very different system from most other social media apps. Therefore, if you're starting out on TikTok, your biggest goal should be to grow your account.

But how exactly can you grow your account?

One of the first things you need to do when starting your business on TikTok is to have a **content plan**. While this might sound very basic, most people never even think about it. According to CoSchedule, creating a good content plan can increase the probability of success in a marketing campaign by **356%** (CoSchedule, 2020).

To achieve this type of success on TikTok, you must include a few things in your content plan.

1. **Set your content marketing goals**: This is an important step in your content plan. It helps you set clear markers to see if you're succeeding or falling short. Setting goals and targets for your TikTok marketing will help you measure growth. Growth can be measure through several metrics. It could be brand awareness, increased sales, a fixed number of additional followers, increased views, more likes and comments, or partnerships with micro-influencers. The goals you set should be realistic, attainable, specific, and measurable within a fixed period. In other words, the goals should be SMART (Specific, Measureable, Attainable, Relevant, and Time-bound). You should gradually adjust your goals higher as you reach them. You should not begin your business on TikTok without knowing what you want to achieve and how you plan to achieve it. Your marketing goals help with this.

2. **Research your target audience:** To succeed on TikTok, you need to understand your target audience's preference clearly. You need to understand what type of content they prefer. Do they prefer Educational or Humorous content? You can achieve this by studying other businesses with a similar target audience or niche. Check out which hashtags, effects, sound, or Challenges they're using. You can also check the videos displayed at the top of each hashtag's search results to understand what type of videos get the most attention.

Don't forget to research your audience by checking the followers of other TikTokers who target them. Find out who they follow, what kind of content they repost, or do duets with.

3. **Choose which content to publish**: TikTok is a social network primarily focused on videos. Although you can post pictures through a slideshow, this won't do too well. According to a 2017 survey by HubSpot Content Trends on over 3000 people from the US, Germany, Colombia, and

Mexico, an average of 54% percent across all age groups show a strong preference for video content. And 52% of respondents ages 18-24 expressed a preference for social videos. This number has increased astronomically since the rise of TikTok and stories on Facebook, Instagram, and WhatsApp (HubSpot, 2020).

If you want your audience to engage with your posts, you need to give them a reason to do so. You need to provide them with the content they want to see. And to understand what they want to see; you need to understand who they are.

To become successful on TikTok, you should have a plan for your intended posts. For example, a Cake designer/baker can post videos showing the process of making and designing cakes, reviews from customers, and instructional videos such as "how to cut a cake evenly." Planning your posts removes the stress of worrying about what to upload every time. And it frees up valuable time for you to focus on other areas of your business. You can also select the songs you intend to use for your videos and keep track of the equipment/tools you might need for your content.

4. Create content to boost engagement: Unless your brand demands perfection, your TikTok videos shouldn't strive for 100% perfection every time. As stated in earlier chapters, for TikTok, quantity is just as important as quality. This is not to encourage substandard content quality but to get you focused on producing lots of content. The golden rule is that all content must be engaging and creative. Spending time obsessing over perfection will slow your growth. You must remember that you're not expected to take yourself too seriously on TikTok; everyone is there to have fun. Your goal is to get discovered on TikTok's "For You" page. This means you only have between 5-10 seconds to make a first impression. Posting content multiple times daily using hashtags increases your chances of your content becoming successful.

5. **Create a Content Calendar:** You need to decide on the frequency of your posts. Business2Community, recommends posting at least 3 times every day. This increases your chance of going viral with one of your posts (Fasulo, 2020). Therefore, having a weekly plan is a way to save yourself the headache of remembering when to post. The content calendar should contain the dates and times for your posts. It should also include the time you will spend researching your target audience, the number of posts you will make each day. The hashtags you intend to use, the content you wish to publish, any micro-influencers you intend to use, and any other relevant information should also be noted.

Don't forget to make unique content on important dates such as holidays/celebrations, special holidays, especially those related to your business, and whenever you launch new products or services. However, you can always make changes and surprises. For example, there could be some big news in your industry that you need to talk about in your post, or perhaps some unforeseen event shocks the world, which could require you to change your tactics.

Take a little time each day to engage with your followers and build stronger relationships by responding to their messages. You can also share and repost other people's content. Have a Livestream from time to time to thank others for shares or nice comments you receive.

Specialized apps like Google Calendar or Google Sheets are fitted with reminders that you can use to create your content calendar instead of writing in notebooks or word documents. You can also use an advanced tool, specifically for TikTok, to help you schedule TikTok posts and manage them directly from the app. An excellent tool for this is tiktokscheduler.com.

Another great tool to use is coschedule.com. CoSchedule is the world's premier management tool for businesses struggling to manage social media accounts, blog posts, events, podcasts, and more. Also, it helps your team reach their full potential by defining priorities and empowering employees to excel in their roles. To get TikTok users interested in your business, you need to be consistent with your content. Having a content calendar helps you achieve that.

6. **Carry out a content audit of your previous post**: To create a content marketing plan, you need an audit to determine your current performance and understand what works and what doesn't. This knowledge will help you build your content strategy.

To complete an audit, you should check for the following:

- Most engaging posts: What posts get the most views, the most shares, the most comments?
- Low-performing posts.
- Post publishing frequency.
- Ranking Hashtags.

7. **Promote your content:** Your content plan should also include your plans to promote your content. On TikTok, content Promotions are paid. However, you can also promote your content by working with influencers and micro-influencers. Promoting your content via email marketing has remained a successful model for most business people, so you should work on growing your email list. Your content plan should include this and your budget for it. While it is important to create engaging content on TikTok, you might also need to promote yourself to grow faster as a small business. According to Derek Halpem of Social Triggers,

content promotion outweighs content creation in importance by 4 to 1 (Social Triggers, 2013).

8. Measure your success and ROI. A perfectly executed content plan should yield good results. Measuring your success in online content marketing includes meeting your SMART goals and executing them. They also include measuring the profit made as a result of these steps. ROI means the Return On investment, and a good ROI means you made a significantly higher amount of money than you spent on executing your content plan. Insights and lessons from your completed goals can then be used to plan your next marketing campaign. You can access your analytics from TikTok to assess the success of your content plan. You can also use other metrics like the number of visits to your online shop or website and the number of new email addresses you collect during the period.

Finally, because of the trend-oriented nature of TikTok, it is a good idea to create a new content plan every week. This makes you much more flexible and able to make amendments and participate in all the trends, hashtags, and viral movements for the week.

CROSS PROMOTING YOUR TIKTOK CONTENT ON OTHER PLATFORMS

TikTok enables all of its users to download and share any content you see on the "For You" feed and the "Following" feed if the content creator grants the permission. This can be done by clicking on the share icon near the bottom-right corner, which brings up some options to share with other TikTok users or on your other social media accounts. It also makes it possible to download the video and save it on your device easily.

. . .

HERE IS what it looks like below:

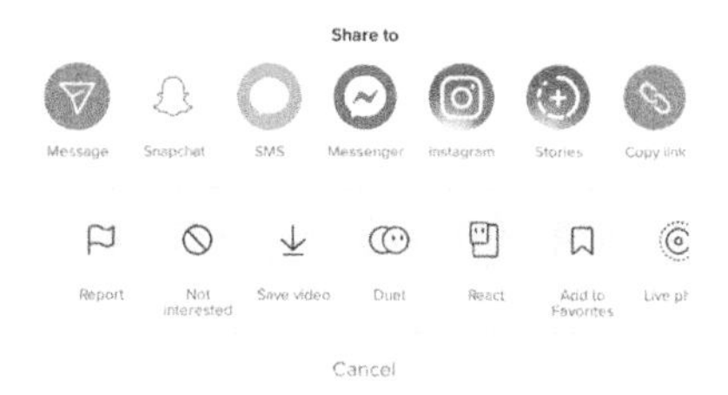

Cross promoting is sharing your content from one social media platform to another. You could share your saved TikTok video on your Twitter, Snapchat, WhatsApp status, Facebook, or Instagram post/story. The 15-second duration for most TikTok videos makes it a perfect fit for Instagram stories. You can add polls and a call to action to encourage your Instagram audience to follow you on TikTok. TikTok's algorithm also loves when you share your content on your other social accounts and will spread your content to a larger group of people.

GROW YOUR ACCOUNT BY ENGAGING WITH OTHER TIKTOK USERS

This section is far more crucial than learning how to market your content. It involves being active on the app and learning how to grow your engagements and interactions organically. As mentioned, a quick way to boost your audience is to partner with TikTok users who share a similar audience with you. This is the fastest way to grow organically because if you make a video by collaborating with other TikTok users, you get engagements from both your account and theirs. It is also an excellent way to make friends and establish valuable relationships.

A great way to engage with other TikTok users is to have duets with them. It works a lot, but you can reach a wider audience if you do it with a popular face on TikTok.

Building relationships on TikTok is usually done by meeting people on the app. You could reach out to other users directly through direct messages or by leaving comments on their posts. You can also attend meetings or conferences that facilitate networking with other content creators. Therefore, to attract someone's attention on TikTok, first leave a comment on their post or engage with their video before sending a direct message. You can also begin your direct messages by complimenting the person on their talents before asking for a partnership. To find meetups or conferences for content creators, you can use websites like www.meetup.com, or you could simply create your own meetup and invite users.

PARTICIPATE IN TRENDS AND CHALLENGES

TikTok thrives on challenges and trends. There are always a lot of challenges that people can participate in at all times. The concept of a TikTok challenge is straightforward: users take an idea, usually started by a TikTok user, and try to replicate it on their videos. An example of a very successful challenge was the 2018 Jimmy Fallon #TumbleweedChallenge. The challenge required users to roll on the ground while playing western music. Today, there are over 12000 #TumbleweedChallenge videos on TikTok, which have been viewed more than 38.3 million times.

For brands or businesses that want to create challenges, TikTok provides official hashtag challenges as an ad displayed for all users in your target location. After a company pays TikTok to start a hashtag challenge, all users can participate in it. However, it is a costly advertising option at over 100,000 dollars.

Alternatively, anyone can start a trend on TikTok and have others participate in them, without paying TikTok anything, although the paid option and partnerships with influencers will inspire more users to participate. When you're starting out on TikTok, you should join in as many trends and challenges as possible and find a way to add details about your business to the videos. These videos are more likely to be recommended to other users, which can boost your viewership and engagement numbers and increase your brand image.

Trends could be in the form of hashtags, sound choices, or effects. You can recognize a trend before it becomes saturated if it shows up 3 times or more on your "For You" page. Follow these trends and explore how you can use them to boost your own business.

HOW TO REACH TIKTOK USERS IN A DIFFERENT COUNTRY

Like most other social media apps, TikTok requires permission to access your location. While most social media apps use the GPS location from your mobile device, TikTok uses the national origin of your SIM card to display content specific to your location, regardless of where you are at the time you're using it. Just as your TikTok feed is restricted to your SIM card's country of origin, your posts are initially shown within your geographic location before being pushed to other areas if they are successful. If you are a business person willing to reach a market in a different country, how do you change your location? An easy way to achieve this is to buy a new SIM card from that country.

CHAPTER FIVE: HOW TO GET THE MOST OUT OF TIKTOK

"You get what you give, but also what you're willing to take."

— **SARAH DESSEN**

As a content creator trying to grow your business on TikTok, you need to continually assess every possible data associated with your posts and accounts. This includes finding out when your videos got the most engagements, which of your videos gets the most likes, comments, and shares, and which videos lead to more sales and increase your email list. The good news is, it is possible to get all this data on TikTok after signing up for the TikTok pro feature.

TikTok Pro is a voluntary feature that can be activated by any user and accessed for free. It was designed for creators and businesses to serve as an analytic tool to help them better understand their performance and engagement. This feature provides insights and overviews on your weekly and monthly views, follower growth, and most successful videos. If you are an aspiring business person on TikTok, it is imperative to activate your account's Pro feature.

Activating the Pro feature on your TikTok account is relatively easy. It only requires answering a few questions. Here is how you can do it: (Sharma Rhimzim,2019)

1. Tap on *"Me"* on the bottom-right of your screen. Click on the options menu on the top right corner (three dots) and click on *"Manage my account."*

2. A 4-option list will be displayed. Click on *"Switch to Pro Account"* highlighted in red at the bottom of the list.

3. You'll then be asked to choose an account type – creator or business. Choose "*Business*" if it's a company account.

4. A list will appear, asking you to choose a category that best describes your content. This will not be displayed publicly.

5. Your account should now be a Pro account, and the *"Business"* option should now be available as a part of your menu. Click on it, and you should be able to open "Analytics."

The picture below illustrates how you can activate your TikTok pro account:

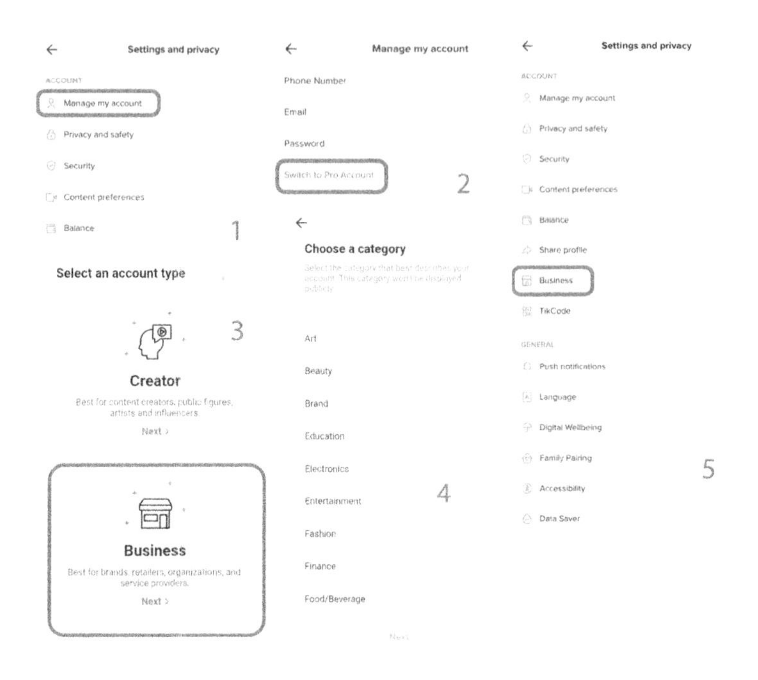

The TikTok Pro account has its benefits. You can monitor all your statistics ranging from a single post to that of a full month (4 weeks). Once you open the Analytics tab, a changeable 7-day *Overview* of your account appears. You can switch between 7 and 28 days. There is a chart representation of video views, followers, and profile views. The *Content* option shows all your posts for the week and which ones are trending on the "For You" page. Finally, *Followers* shows insights into the number of followers you have and your followers' gender ratio, among others. Check your progress regularly. If you use a PC, you can download it as a CSV file.

Insights are also available per post. They show the *total watch time, total views, average time watched, traffic source, and audience overview.* Audience overview offers the total views your video has and where your viewers found the content you uploaded. These numbers are displayed in percentages. For example, 79% found it on the "For You" page. *Traffic Source* shows you the countries/locations of your content viewers. It also displays it in percentages (Later Media,2020).

HOW TO DETERMINE YOUR PERFORMANCE ON TIKTOK

If you are a young girl starting your business on TikTok, you need to check your posts' progress regularly. Your performance on TikTok is best assessed by looking at the increase in watch time, the average watch time for your posts, and the number of new followers you gain. Your TikTok shares, comments, and likes might not be the best way to judge your progress, especially when you start out. While shares, comments, and likes are important; watch time is the most critical factor for assessing your growth. It is also the most intrinsically connected to TikTok's algorithms. Therefore, an increase in your watch time shows your content is getting more users engaged, and your fan base is growing. This will expand your brand awareness, which should be the biggest goal for a new business. You could also compare your number of follow to the previous period and monitor the increase over a number of videos or time.

COMMON REASONS WHY POSTS DON'T GET ENOUGH VIEWS

1. You may be shadowbanned. The simplest definition for the "shadow ban" is limiting your content reach by restricting visibility without any notification from the platform that your content is violating community guidelines or usage rules.

2. Poor engagement on previous videos.

3. Using an outdated trending sound or song.

4. The video lacks creativity, humor, or value.

5. Bad timing: posting when your audience is inactive.

6. Using a banned hashtag or topic. This means using something that flouts TikTok's guidelines.

7. Posting from a new account without liking or sharing any content.

8. The video doesn't have a hook or title to engage people in the first 2 seconds.

QUICK WAYS TO FIX THE PROBLEMS

1. Re-edit the video and re-publish it. Change the transitions, song, or cut it differently to make the video more appealing.

2. Make videos that your audience can relate to and will be moved to share with others on TikTok and other social media platforms.

3. Be authentic and fun. People can detect if you're doing it for the money or trying to copy other people.

4. Refrain from deleting videos on your TikTok unless the views on the video make up less than 1% of your following. Frequent deletion leads to TikTok tagging your account as having a high rate of poor-performing videos. TikTok gives content a second chance at going viral, so don't delete any of your old posts until after a 2-week minimum period. It's common for videos to take time before they take off and go viral.

5. Increase your watch time by encouraging people to watch to the end. Use looped videos – videos in which the beginning and the end look the same, post shorter videos – around 12 seconds – at least two times a day for a higher chance of being promoted by TikTok. You can also entice people into watching more of your content by offering different parts of the same content to encourage people to open your profile and watch the rest of it. Encourage your audience to comment on your videos – while commenting, the videos keep playing in the background, which increases watch time. Also, more comments per video boosts the video's performance. Lastly, engage your commenters to encourage lasting conversations.

HOW TO BECOME VERIFIED ON TIKTOK

Getting verified on TikTok, as simple as it may sound, cannot be achieved unless you're a celebrity or a very popular brand, business, or organization. Verified accounts are identified by the blue checkmark next to their user ID. Being verified confirms that the account name belongs to the user. Making your normal TikTok account verified requires meeting a series of TikTok requirements. More active accounts have a higher chance of becoming verified. Also, while your account must engage other users with interesting media, it is vital never to violate any of the TikTok terms and conditions.

Besides popular celebrities, TikTok users with a massive following can also become verified. Use one or more of the following guidelines to get your account verified:

1. You must have a *consistently growing following*. You could offer incentives to make a lot of users follow you. Incentives like giveaways and follow backs (Rachel Pederson, 2020).

2. Have *a growing watch time and views*. This will only happen when you post popular content. The time people spend on your videos, the number of viewers you receive per post, and the engagement levels should increase every day.

3. *Work with the media, press, or public relations.* Your followers and other TikTok users – the general TikTok community – must be able to verify that you have been featured or work with some popular media outlets like TV shows, magazines, newspapers, and others.

4. *Create consistently viral content.* You should have at least one viral content per week to prove you have become a major "influencer" and not just any ordinary TikTok user. While this may not be easy to achieve, especially when you're starting

out, you can aspire to achieve at least one viral post per month and gradually increase it (Rachel Pederson, 2020) (Joshua Crumpley, 2020).

5. It speeds things up if you *have verifications on other social media platforms*. Having a verified account on other platforms like Facebook, Instagram, and Twitter would improve your chances of getting verified on TikTok.

6. *Use TikTok ads*. In the next chapter, TikTok ads and paid promotions will be highlighted. A TikTok ad costs a minimum of six thousand dollars, and it can be upwards of one hundred and fifty thousand dollars for a daily ad campaign. Frequent use of TikTok ads, especially past the fifty thousand dollar mark, increases your chances of getting your verified badge quickly (Later Media, 2020).

7. If you are an unverified popular brand, *reach out to TikTok* to get verified to protect your authenticity.

THE FUTURE OF TIKTOK

Using TikTok for your business means you should always be ready to capitalize on any new additions to the app. Therefore, you should anticipate any future features that might appear on TikTok and prepare your business to take advantage of them. In *Chapter 1*, this book explored the history of TikTok and its relationship with ***Douyin.*** Douyin and TikTok are both owned by ByteDance, a Chinese tech company that is the most valuable startup in the world. TikTok and Douyin are almost identical in every way. The main difference is that TikTok operates in markets outside China, while Douyin serves the Chinese market. This difference provides an astonishing amount of innovative edge to Douyin, which enables it to add lots of additional features without running afoul of the many regulatory restrictions in many countries of the world. It also serves as a sort of testing platform to see what works before release to the global TikTok app. Therefore, you can anticipate future TikTok features by looking at what Douyin currently offers.

Douyin is more advanced than TikTok, especially in areas around e-commerce. For example, a mind-blowing feature on Douyin is the ability to **book a room in a hotel or Airbnb room where the video you're watching was shot.** You can do this without leaving the video you're watching. So if you like the hotel or Airbnb you see on a video, you simply have to tap on it and go to the hotel booking website.

Douyin also facilitates **social commerce**. It offers its users the opportunity to buy products featured on a video. You could buy an item shown in a video by simply clicking on it. For example, if you're watching a video and seeing a cosmetic product you like, you simply have to click on the product and an e-commerce link – like Amazon – will pop up so you can buy it easily. Many tech experts consider this the future of online shopping. However, it is not yet available on any major social media apps outside China (Manish Singh,2019).

Another interesting feature is **virtual tours of stores and restaurants in videos** posted by the store/restaurant or any TikTok user who feels like providing it. All the goods in the store have their prices and web-links hyperlinked to the video, and you can click on any product you want to buy them from the store's website and have them delivered. A similar process is possible with restaurants and Cafes. You can click on an item and have it delivered to your doorstep. All from the Douyin app (Josh Ye, 2020).

Furthermore, *Douyin* makes it possible to leave reviews of places you see in another user's video. This could serve as a kind of free promotion or advertisement for businesses shown in videos. You could easily find the location of the place you are watching by clicking on it, which automatically takes you to their exact location on a map app – similar to how it works on

Google Maps – where you can leave reviews. This feature is referred to as **geotagging** (Jeremy Goldkorn, 2019).

Douyin's most intriguing feature is probably the **in-video facial recognition search.** Instead of the traditional method of searching for a TikTok user, you can activate an in-video facial search to show you the user in a video before proceeding to view more content from that person. However, this feature might take some time to be adopted by western markets due to privacy concerns (Adan Kohnhorst, 2019).

The final feature from Douyin that we'll be examining is **full feature films.** This feature was introduced during China's Corona Virus (COVID-19) lockdown, a period in which all public places, including cinemas, were shut. *Douyin* decided to make it possible for its users to watch full films on the app. Some international movies like *The Great Wall* starring Matt Damon, the Academy Award-winning *The Last Emperor,* and acclaimed Cannes Film Festival favorite, *Farewell My Concubine,* were all made available alongside local Chinese movies. A highly anticipated film, *"Lost in Russia,"* premiered on *Douyin* after they paid $90.8 million to acquire the film's rights. And because it couldn't be shown in cinemas across the country, Douyin users embraced it.

However, while some of these innovations are likely coming to TikTok soon, others might face extreme scrutiny from Western governments. The innovations around social commerce and e-commerce can provide considerable benefits to both small and large businesses. The key is to produce compelling videos that can attract many TikTok viewers, who will then buy the products from your online store, leave their reviews on your page, or pay for lodging in your hotel/Airbnb. The movie industry could also benefit significantly from these features because it would bring movies to the most addictive social platform for young people at a time when the COVID-19 pandemic is devastating traditional cinemas (Sekhar Maddala, 2020).

CHAPTER SIX: REACH YOUR CUSTOMERS THROUGH TIKTOK ADS

"All Advertising is essentially a promise of future happiness."

— **SULEMAN ABDULLAH**

LIKE MOST OTHER SOCIAL MEDIA APPS, TIKTOK OFFERS advertising products to assist businesses and creators in reaching millions of other TikTok users worldwide. The TikTok ad manager, similar to Facebook and Instagram's ad manager, allows you to target the exact people your business or brand needs to increase sales. It makes it possible to micro-target to your specific target audience. It is also possible to reach a *"Lookalike audience,"* which are other people with similar qualities or tastes to your target audience. There are 5 types of TikTok ads. They are *brand takeovers, in-feed ads, branded hashtag challenge, branded effects, and a "top-view" video*. Most brands begin their ad campaigns on TikTok with branded hashtag challenges. These can be found on the *"Discovery"* page of the TikTok app. The number of times content from hashtag has been viewed worldwide is also displayed. You can make your TikTok ad "subscription" daily, weekly or lifetime. It is not fixed, and it can be changed anytime during your campaign to fit your budget. Furthermore, TikTok runs ads for all types of brands/businesses except controversial companies selling alcohol, tobacco, and other harmful products.

Before beginning your ad campaign, it is crucial to know which type of ad suits your brand or business. Therefore, here is a detailed explanation of each of the ads.

IN-FEED ADS

In-Feed Ads are video ads that appear in between user videos as you browse the "For You" page. They are similar to ads seen while swiping through Instagram stories tagged "Sponsored." They can span between 9 to 15 seconds, leaving you enough time to express your message as creatively as possible. You could also add call-to-action to the videos like an encouragement to download your app or visit your website or buy your products/shop with you.

In-Feed Ads can be scrolled past very quickly, leaving you 2 to 3 seconds to catch your audience's attention. In-Feed Ads should be full screen and captivating enough to stop TikTok users from scrolling past it. You could work with influencers to do a better job of grabbing attention. A positive benefit to In-Feed Ads is that users viewing it can leave a like, comment, share, and interact with your video. It is also important that the video's text be exciting enough to get users to turn on the sound – for users with muted sounds. An example of an In-Feed Ads is an Adobe Lightroom In-Feed Ad with a clear Call to Action (CTA) asking you to download the app (Jessica Worb, 2020).

BRAND TAKEOVER ADS

Have you ever opened your TikTok app and seen an ad immediately? Those are Brand Takeover Ads. Brand Takeover Ads appear immediately upon opening the app, presenting a full-screen video to its target audience.

Brand Takeovers are probably the best ad options. Your content is placed right under the noses of your target audience, delivering mass awareness and direct sales for your business. Not only do they take over your potential customer's screen upon launching the app, but they also appear in between videos on the "For You" page as images. GIFs or videos include a clickable link to the brand's website or a sales website for direct purchase. They can also encourage users to participate in a hashtag challenge on TikTok.

TikTok has designed its app to ensure no account receives more than one Brand Takeover Ad per day. This means you can reach out to a vast audience with little or no competition. However, Brand Takeovers are not the best option for a first-timer because they are very expensive. Larger brands or companies with budgets big enough to accommodate the high cost can attract many customers using them, especially those seeking younger customers.

Here is an example of a Nike brand takeover ad. You can skip the ad by tapping on "Skip ads" at the top right corner of your screen or wait till it plays out (Influencer Marketing Hub, 2020).

TOP VIEW ADS

This is a new ad option built on the foundations of the Brand Takeover Ad. The difference is that Top View Ads – unlike Brand Takeover Ads – don't overwhelm the target audience as soon as they open up their TikTok app. Top View Ads appear as the first video. The Top View Ads play for up to 60 seconds on a full screen (Jessica Worb, 2020).

BRANDED HASHTAG CHALLENGE

This is an advertising medium exclusive to TikTok. Like regular hashtags, branded hashtags offer both organic and sponsored opportunities for brands. It is an excellent way to build brand awareness and to generate content from other TikTok users. The branded Hashtag can be fun. It allows the brands to be integrated into the TikTok society by collaborating with influencers, TikTok users, and even other brands.

Branded Hashtags provide a way for brands to get maximum exposure, grow their TikTok accounts, and improve sales. Hashtag challenges are costly and are, therefore, left for the largest brands to run. An example is the #therealfreal used to introduce the F'real Milkshake from Oreo. Since the campaign, their TikTok account has grown to almost seven hundred thousand followers, with over two hundred million hashtag video views.

TikTok now offers an additional feature to the Hashtag Challenge, called the Hashtag Challenge Plus. The Hashtag Challenge Plus allows users to shop for products directly from the TikTok app – via e-commerce. This additional feature has only been activated on a few accounts (as of September 2020). It offers a separate "Discover" tab on the Hashtag page where

TikTok users can browse the brand or company's products. (Sarah Perez, 2019)

BRANDED EFFECTS

TikTok offers branded and shareable sticker collections, AR filters, and lenses under their advertisement options. Just like Snapchat lenses, these stickers can be used to advertise in an enjoyable way. It allows brands to use the ad to design a custom sticker for themselves. They could be live for up to 10 days encouraging interaction with the brand. An example is this ad by the Coco Chanel brand. Their lenses and sticker packs allow TikTok users to wear a virtual cosmetic look while simultaneously representing the brand (Andrew Hutchinson, 2020).

EXAMPLES OF SUCCESSFUL ADS ON TIKTOK

There have been numerous widely successful ads on TikTok over the years. Many brands and companies have come to TikTok to attract more people to their businesses – especially brands trying to reach millennials and Gen Z – or promote brand awareness. A lot of them opt to use TikTok ads, which usually pay off eventually. Examples of very successful ads are the Guess #InMyDenim hashtag challenge and the Chipotle #tiktoktimeout challenge.

Guess, the popular denim and lifestyle brand launched its ad on TikTok on September 1st, 2018 running it through September 6. During the 6-day campaign, TikTok users were taken directly to the #InMyDenim hashtag challenge. The videos featured influencers and TikTok users transforming their appearances from being unpresentable in the "Before" to glamourous in the "After" featuring apparel from Guess (Gabriella Lacombe, 2018).

The Chipotle #tiktoktimeout was sponsored by the Mexican fast-food restaurant, Chipotle Mexican Grill (CMG). The sponsor collaborated with mega influencers on TikTok. People with millions of followers like:

- Zach King – 27.2 million followers
- Brent Rivera – 16 million followers
- David Dobrik – 6.4 million followers
- Brittany Browski – 2 million followers
- Avani Gregg – 25.3 million followers
- Nick Uhas – 7.4 million followers
- Zahra – 2.7 million followers

These influencers were asked to make personal content videos set to Justin Beiber's hit song "Yummy" and incorporating Chipotle. It was also meant to raise public awareness about Chipotle's free delivery offer for purchases exceeding $10 in February. The ad campaign was a smashing success, and Chipotle's TikTok account now stands at over 1.2 million followers.

So how do you create a TikTok Ads account? Simple! Log on to the TikTok ads website - https://www.tiktok.com/business/en and click on the "Get started" button. A form will pop up requesting details to set up your account.

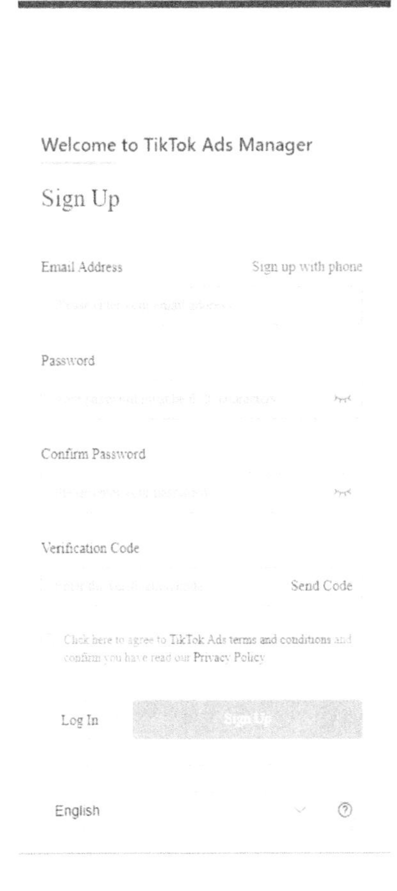

OVERVIEW OF THE TIKTOK ADS MANAGER

The TikTok Ads interface provides 4 tabs to choose from once logged in. From left to right, there's *Dashboard, Campaign, Assets,* and *Reporting.*

The **Dashboard** is the first stop on the TikTok Ads Manager. It provides an overview of your data, and it makes it possible to track performance changes. It is the right place to get a perfect view of your ad campaign's progress. It contains summarized data – budget spent, active campaign(s), and charts tracking the active campaign(s) over time, among other features.

Clicking on the **Campaign** tab shows all the ad campaigns, ad groups, and ads you have created, alongside budget, total cost, impressions, clicks, conversions, click rate, conversion rate, CPC, CPM, and conversion cost. It also features a "Create" option to begin a new campaign, which will simply take you to the ad creation page.

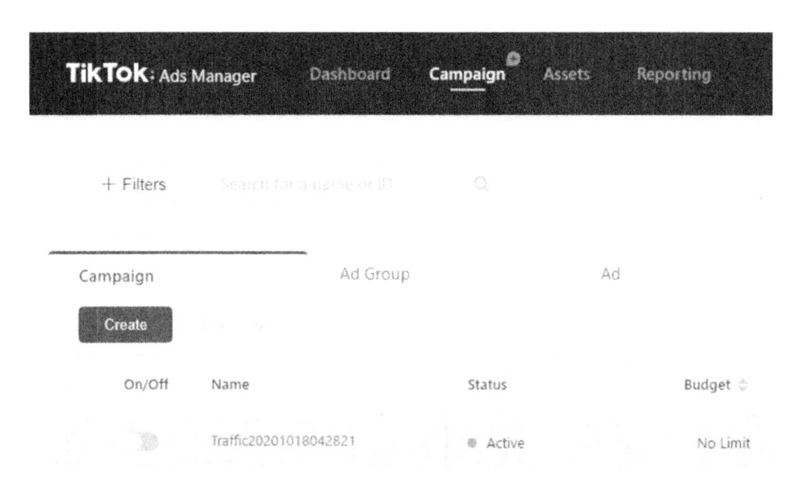

On the **Assets** page, you can manage events tabs used to track in-app conversions and website events. The creative tab allows you to create and manage creative content. You can also upload your playable ad(s).

A playable ad is an interactive ad format that provides a short, engaging experience attracting users and getting them to download your app or game—finally, the audience tab allows you to upload files containing information about your custom audience.

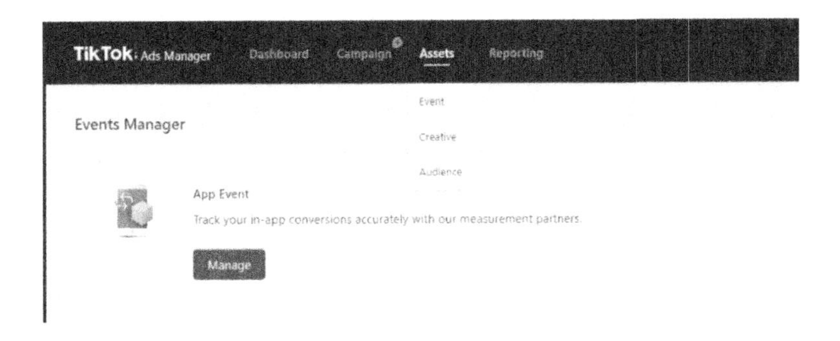

The **Reporting** area is where you go to see your results from the ad campaign. You can customize your ads report by creating a report template, and the TikTok Ads manager will automatically produce all your reports that way. Ads reports can also be scheduled to delivered at any time you choose.

HOW TO SET UP A TIKTOK AD CAMPAIGN

Create an Ad Campaign

Running an ad starts with creating a "Campaign." Log into your Ads account on the TikTok Ads site. Click on "Campaign" and then click on "Create" to begin the process. This is the part where you determine the campaign's objectives or goals, which involves determining the outcome you expect at the end of the campaign. The campaign objective is the most important decision you must make because it impacts all other decisions around your ad campaign. There are five main ad objectives you can choose from:

- *Reach:* This is the option for businesses aiming to make as many impressions as possible. It is excellent for improving brand awareness, especially for big companies like Coca-Cola or Pepsi.
- *Video Views:* Select this as your objective if your ad is aimed at getting as many people as possible to watch your full TikTok video.
- *App Installs:* Here, the objective is to get many people to download and install your company's app. To successfully do this, you need a third-party attribution partner like Adjust or Appsfire.
- *Traffic:* This is the option for TikTok users or brands/companies trying to draw traffic to their websites or online store.
- *Conversions:* More than just drawing attention to your website, if you want those people to take action on your website, like to buy your products or to sign up for your newsletter, this is the objective for you. This ad objective targets customers willing to pay.

After choosing one of them, you can select a split test option, running two campaigns where only one variable is different. For example, you might intend to run two different ads concurrently for the same country. TikTok uses split testing to compare the results of the two ads and chooses the best performing campaign. Alternatively, if you do not decide to use an automatic split test, you could run two separate ads simultaneously and turn off the one that does not perform well with your target audience.

Manual split testing can be used to test various target audiences using the same creative, or it can test two different creatives using the same target audience, for example, running two ad groups, one for the US and the other for the UK.

Each ad campaign can include more ad groups, and each ad group can consist of more ads or videos. Creating more videos for each ad campaign will allow the algorithm to decide which ones perform the best and allocate a higher budget percentage for them. The process for this is called split testing.

Finally, enter a name for the ad campaign, then put in your budget for the ad. The minimum should be $50.00. There is also the option to select a lifetime budget by checking the "No Limit" box.

Set up an Ad Group

This determines how your ads will run. It involves targeting the right users and bidding process. There can be one or multiple ads under one ad group, enabling you to compare all those ads' delivery and optimize them to improve their performance. You can set up an ad group following these basic steps:

- Choose a placement option

- Fill in ad details

- Set your target audience

▾ Demographics

Location

United States ×

The actual ads delivery may vary depending on the supported locations of different placements. Learn more

Gender

No Limit Male Female

Age

No Limit 13-17 18-24 25-34 35-44 45-54 55+

Languages

English ×

- Check "Automated Creative Optimization"

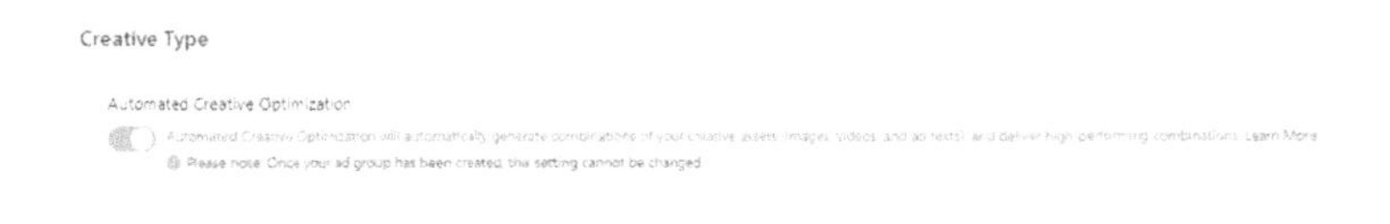

- Set up a budget and schedule

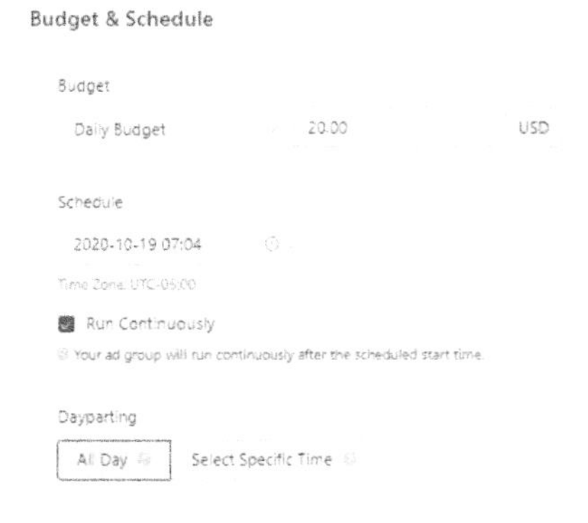

- Set optimization goals and bidding method

Other Ways to Set your Target Audience

There are 3 ways to target your dream customers.

- *Interest Based*: Target people based on their selected interests on TikTok. It is easy to achieve this on TikTok because TikTok knows each user's based on the kind of content they consume. This is the least efficient way to target users.

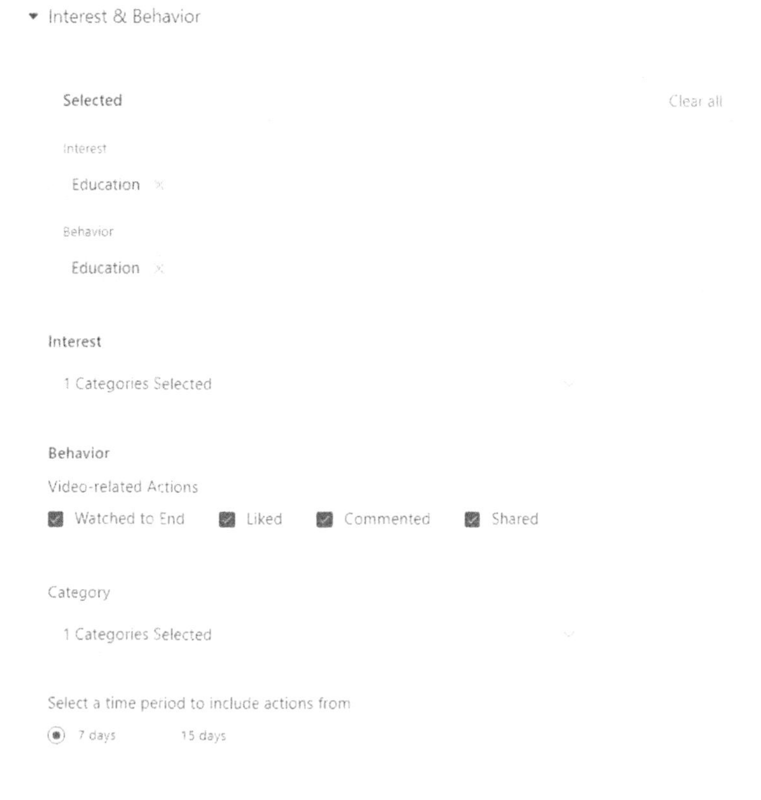

- *Custom Audience*: This is the most efficient way to get your target audience. Custom audiences are people who have engaged with your business or your content. And Lookalike audiences are people with similar characteristics to your custom audience, but are different users.

▾ Audience

Included

Optional

Excluded

Optional

- *Demographic*: Target people based on their location, age, gender or language. The efficiency of this method is average. But it is far more efficient than merely targeting by interest because most people usually have multiple conflicting interests.

Finally, combining the above ways would be most efficient way to successfully target your audience. You can start by targeting based on demographics and interests. After you have completed your initial ad campaign, you can begin your subsequent campaigns by choosing a custom audience.

HOW TO CREATE CUSTOM AND LOOKALIKE AUDIENCES ON TIKTOK

- *Creating a custom audience*: There are 4 ways to do this.
- Upload a custom file that includes all your customers (name, email addresses) and tell TikTok to target those users.

- If you have an app, connect it to TikTok to target all the people interacting with the app.

- *Creating a lookalike audience*

You need to have a custom audience of at least 10,000 people to create a lookalike audience. When creating a lookalike audience, there are three options to choose from based on your niche. If your niche is specific, choose "Narrow."

- Broad – users that are a match for your custom audience in a broad sense
- Balanced – users with similar characteristics to your custom audience.
- Narrow – users that are as similar as possible to your custom audience.

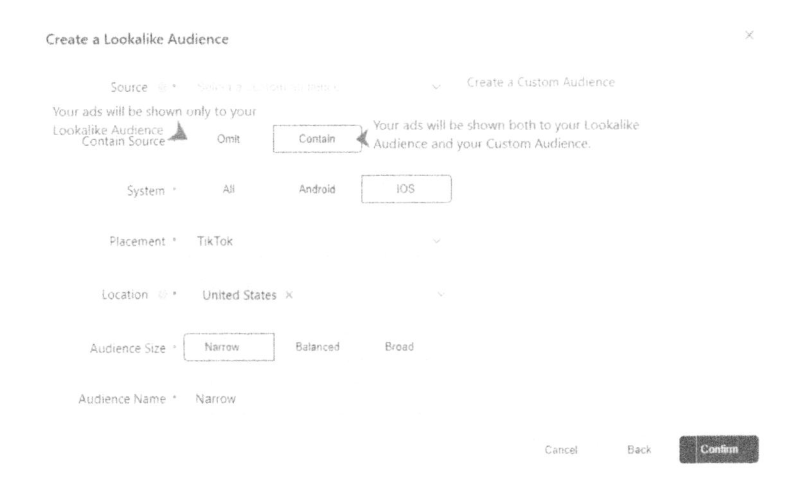

Other Ad Group Settings

These settings can be switched on and off and can be customized to suit your desire. There are six major settings. Here is the breakdown:

- *Ad Placement:* This allows the content creator to choose where they want the ad to be displayed. This system is called select placement. TikTok also makes it possible to place ads automatically. Ad placement directly influences the ad's reach, and automatic ad placement allows ad delivery across TikTok and its related apps (Vigo Video, Buzz Video, Top Buzz, and News Republic).
- Basic information about what you're advertising. The information on every ad is crucial to the ad having a good ROI. It has to be short, precise, and captivating enough to boost the ad's performance. Basic information includes the type of promotion such as app install or website, the display name, the profile image, and the ad's category, among others.

Furthermore, "User comment" and "Video download" allow other TikTok users to make comments and download your ad video, respectively. These can be activated or deactivated, depending on your needs.

- Tags or keywords help the algorithm match the right users to your business or TikTok account. The limit is set at 20 tags.
- *Creative optimization*: This option allows your creative content to be matched with different headlines to find the right combination that performs best. The system uses your creative assets, including images, videos, and ad text to find these combinations.
- *Daily Budget*: Your ad budget for a day can be set in the Ad Group. The daily minimum budget in an Ad Group is $20. The amount set for a day is not necessarily exhausted daily, but it ensures that the amount of money used every day does not exceed the fixed amount. It is better to start with as low an amount as possible and scale up the amount if the ad campaign performs well.
- *Smart optimization:* This allows you to decide how the system optimizes conversion events and conducts smart delivery. It is important for the efficient delivery of the ad. Bid strategy controls the cost per result. Standard bid controls the result more strictly, so the average CPR stays within your bid all through the campaign.
- *Bidding Settings*: This is used to set the amount you're willing to pay per thousand impressions, per click, or per conversion. The TikTok algorithm delivers your ads based on your bids either by the "Standard" option or "Accelerate" option. The standard option spends your scheduled budget evenly throughout the

campaign, while the Accelerate option spends it as quickly as possible.

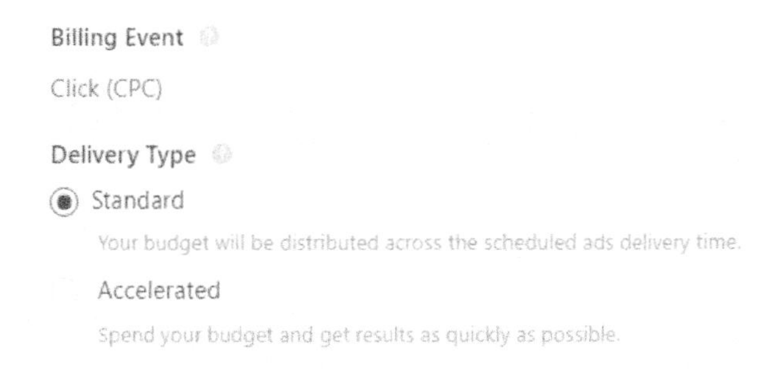

- *Third-party tracking system settings:* This helps monitor ad performance and attributions using apps other than TikTok.

Create your ads

Ads are the contents you present to the target audience for them to see on their TikTok apps. Your ad content could be in image or video form. TikTok Ads Manager is equipped with video creation tools to help you create engaging videos for your ads, even if you do not have any prior knowledge of video editing.

Set up your ad in two basic steps:

- Upload your images or videos
- Add text, including copy and call-to-action buttons

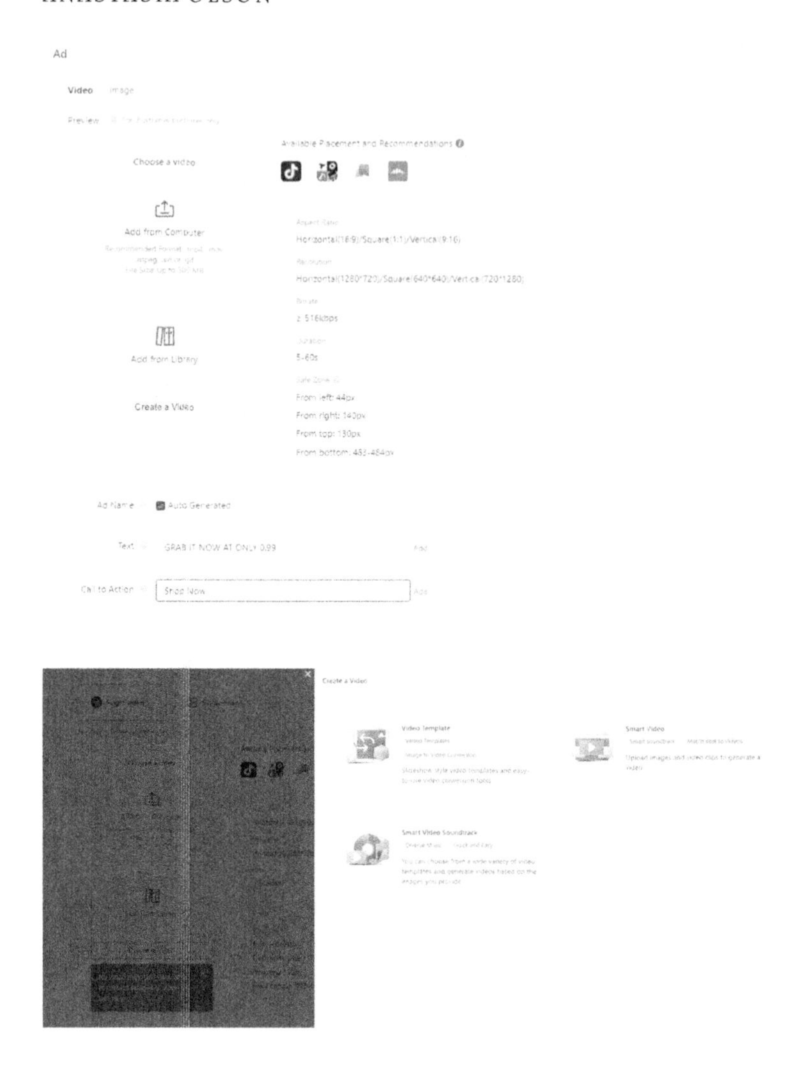

TikTok is a video-based platform, so images don't perform as well as videos. So, what should your video content be like?

1. Your ad video should be shot vertically, so it's full screen on the audience's devices.

2. Keep the video short and detailed enough to attract users' attention within a short time.

3. Create "organic" videos – they perform better than regular ads. People easily recognize ads, and they will be filtered out unless it doesn't look like one.

4. Use people that look like your target audience in your ads. It helps to establish trust between the audience and the content's message.

5. If you don't have a video for the ad, use a template to create a slideshow of pictures. This won't perform as well as videos.

HOW LONG TO WAIT FOR YOUR AD PRICES TO STABILIZE

Starting a campaign puts the TikTok Ads algorithm in a learning phase to determine what users are the best match for your products. It takes more time when you are starting out. You will need up to 50 optimization events (add to cart) before exiting the learning phase. The Cost Per Action (CPA) might be 20% to 30% higher than average during the learning phase.

EVALUATING THE PERFORMANCE OF YOUR ADS

The general rule of thumb is that 90 out of 100 ads a person runs will fail, 7 might break even, which means they neither bring profit nor loss, and 3 will do very well. Of these 3, one or two might perform well enough to be scaled up for a long time.

Should your ad fail to perform well, you need to know when to "kill" or "not kill" it. How do you know if the ad has failed? Look at the Click Through Rate (CTR). If your CTR is lower than your average, the ad has failed to entice the target audience, or the video is not interesting enough. You should **kill the ad** as soon as possible and review why the ad has failed. Also, kill the ad if it has very little engagement and zero or unexpectedly low conversions. A performing ad, on the other hand, will have the opposite performance.

An ad might be presented as failed when some internal or external factors are out of place. It could be the effect of macro events or normal fluctuation. This is why it is vital to check your weekly data to see which days yielded good results and which did not.

Your ad could also appear like they have failed if you have targeted the wrong audience. Thoroughly research your audience repeatedly and look for excellent content that captures their interests. This would help you avoid burning through your budget without a good ROI. If you have a situation in which the CTR of the ad is good, and there are no obvious macro events, but the ad still fails, it is also a sign of wrong a target audience. Test out different types of targeting until you find the best performing one.

Leave an ad running if it breaks even. This means the profit generated from sales equals that ad's budget. Give it some time to yield a profit. Monitor these ads closely and "kill" them immediately if the ad budget exceeds the sales profit.

The best solution for finding high performing ads is to run multiple ads, like 100. Don't worry about spending too much. You can quickly see which ads don't work well and "kill" them. The best performing ads of the remaining will compensate for the money lost during the testing.

Scaling up an ad simply means increasing the budget associated with it and expanding its audience. You should consider scaling up an ad once you hit more than 5 sales within a short period. This will help you reach and attract more customers (TeeSpring Community, 2019-2020).

ADS REPORTING

To create a report of your ad campaign for evaluation, simply click on "Create" under the "Reporting" tab on the homepage of the TikTok Ads Manager after you have logged in, of course. However, if you wish to create a custom report, you can do this by following the steps below:

1. On the reporting page, click on "Create" and then on "Custom Report" from the list of options that appears.

2. The "Custom Report" page will show a list of *Dimensions* and *Metrics* on the left side. "Dimensions" controls data grouping. They appear as rows in the report. Examples include age, gender, ads, ad group, and campaign. "Metrics," on the other hand, are related to ad performance data like the CTR. They appear as columns in the report. Select the data you desire on your ad report.

3. Select the time frame you want on the report.

4. Click on "Save" and rename the report.

If you want to avoid exporting reports manually every time, activate the "Schedule Running" feature to automatically receive reports in your mail periodically.

HOW THE ADS AUCTION WORKS

All ads function as an auction. You are in never-ending competition with other companies for people's attention. The more you pay, the higher the quality of customers you might attract.

The cost of an ad is affected by several variables. Prices vary based on the characteristics of your target audience. If your target audience is Americans, it will cost you more money than targeting an Eastern European audience. Big events like financial crises or a pandemic can also influence the price.

Generally, newer platforms charge less for marketing and ads than established social media companies. Therefore, a relatively new social media platform like TikTok probably charges less for ads than, say, Instagram. Other factors that affect the price of an ad are micro variables. For example, if an ad engages more people to watch it, the bidding price will be lower.

How do you calculate your bid?

The first thing to calculate is the *Customer Acquisition Cost (CAC)*. This is the cost of getting a single customer. A second figure is the *Lifetime Value (LTV)*, which is the amount of revenue generated from one customer on average. For example, if 10 people visit your website and only one bought goods for $10, the LTV is $1 per customer.

You need to monitor your CAC to LTV ratio. This ratio determines if the ad being run is yielding results or if it is a waste of money and resources. The ratios can be interpreted as follows:

- If **CAC** *is less than* **LTV** = You're making a profit.
- If **CAC** *is equals to* **LTV** = You're breaking even.
- If **CAC** *is greater than* **LTV** = You're losing money.

You need to set a daily budget for your advertisements. Having a low bid will give other brands or competitors a chance to outbid you and acquire your potential customers (Brian Kotlyar, 2018).

SPYING ON THE COMPETITION TO TAKE INSPIRATION FROM THEIR AD VIDEOS

One way to select the ad you want to run is by checking your competitors' successful ads. Go to the Facebook ad library and search for the company operating within your niche. Check out all the ads they've run. Filter these ads by the targeted country and platforms. The aim is not to copy these ads but to see what works and what doesn't so you can learn from them. Sort the ads by impressions and then by the platform. You should be especially interested in Instagram stories. The best performing ads will be the ones repeated over and over again.

After checking out these ads, take note of every aspect of the ad. The sound clips, the video quality, the concept, how they offer their products, and the call to action. Try to replicate these with your ads without copying them. Your goal should be to improve on the creativity of your competitors and offer something better to your target audience (Daniel Sandoval, 2020).

facebook ads library

All Images Videos News Books More Settings Tools

About 406,000,000 results (0.60 seconds)

www.facebook.com › ads › library

Ad Library - Facebook

Facebook's advertising tools might not work as expected when an **ad** blocker is enabled in a web browser. Turn off the **ad** blocker or add this web page's URL as ...

Library
The ad library is a place where you can search for ads that are ...

API
The Ad Library application programming interface (API ...

Political Ad Library
Ad LibraryThe ad library provides advertising transparency by ...

Report
Candidates must have a Facebook Page to appear in the spending ...

Ad Library Report
Candidates must have a Facebook Page to appear in the spending ...

More results from facebook.com »

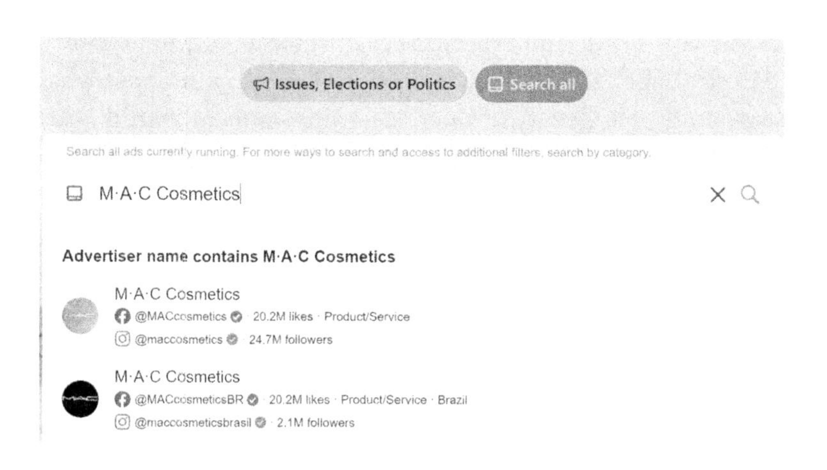

CHAPTER SEVEN: WORKING WITH TIKTOK INFLUENCERS

"The most influential people you will ever meet were once held together by the encouragement of others."

— **SHANNON L. ALDER**

TikTok influencers are a group of social media influencers that have transformed the world of business. This new marketing strategy presumes that a person with a network of people can help market a brand. It functions on the premise that people are more likely to trust a product or brand if it is endorsed by someone they follow or admire. Some of the world's biggest social media influencers are the Kardashian/Jenner family, who earn millions for a single post on their TikTok or Instagram pages.

On TikTok, influencers can help you take your brand to people you would otherwise not be able to reach. And because TikTok primarily functions via quality videos, influencers will most likely be more experienced in presenting your brand to your potential customers in captivating ways. So what separates TikTok influencers from other TikTok users? The primary measure for determining who qualifies as a TikTok influencer is the person's number of followers and engagement frequency. TikTok influencers typically have between hundreds of thousands to millions of followers. To achieve this kind of followership on TikTok requires consistently churning out engaging content or prior fame, like Justin Bieber or Will Smith.

TikTok influencers can help you directly target potential customers for your business. While it is true that some people buy a lot of followers, real TikTok influencers usually have dedicated followers, and influencers succeed because of the trust they built with their followers over a long period. This is precisely why an endorsement from these social influencers can bring considerable benefits to your business.

However, the idea of an "influencer" did not start with TikTok or any other social media app. Someone like Oprah Winfrey has long been considered one of the biggest influencers of all time. For example, in 2015, she bought a stake in Weight Watchers, and the company saw an 83% stock market increase within a few hours. Her endorsement of Barack Obama in early 2008 also contributed to him becoming president.

AN EXAMPLE OF A SUCCESSFUL INFLUENCE CAMPAIGN

Businesses around the world are remaking their marketing budgets to include TikTok influencers. These businesses are capitalizing on the opportunities provided by TikTok to reach consumers across the globe. There are numerous examples of big companies using influencers to reach new customers on TikTok. Many TikTok celebrities have also used this strategy to climb the ladder to success. A prime example of a successful influencer marketing strategy on TikTok is the #PMTurns40 Campaign.

#PMTurns40 is an advertising campaign by Paul Mitchell, a global leader in the hair care and hair product industry. With more than eighty products in the market today, the company is celebrating its 40th anniversary in 2020. Paul Mitchel launched the #PMTurns40 challenge, which, according to the company's statement: "this yearlong celebration will honor our passion for helping people, the products that make you feel great every day, and our commitment to caring for the planet."

The #PMTurns40 challenge was not only made for TikTok but posted across all social media, including Facebook and Instagram. The challenge's central idea was to get people to style their hair similar to how it was done in the 80s, 90s, or early 2000s. Set to the song: *Flip It - (Paul Mitchell)* by Wiidope featuring Adanna Duru, it became a smashing success garnering over 9.6 million views as of September 2020.

The #PMTurns40 challenge became a success not just because Paul Mitchell paid influencers to participate in it. It was successful because many regular TikTok users participated in the challenge, following the influencers' footsteps. This is an example of the power of influencer marketing.

WHY SHOULD YOU WORK WITH TIKTOK INFLUENCERS?

There are lots of benefits you can derive from using TikTok influencers to promote your brand. Some of them are highlighted below:

1. Helps to build brand trust

TikTok influencers can help in building a strong relationship between your brand and your customers. This is because it makes them more likely to trust your brand, which is one of the most critical aspects of consumer marketing. If people trust your brand, they are not only likely to buy your products once; they are liable to buy it over and over again, becoming loyal customers in the future.

2. Enhances brand awareness

One of the most exciting benefits of connecting with a TikTok influencer is that they help create strong brand awareness. They possess an ability to reach a broader range of people than would otherwise be possible. They are also more likely to create viral content, which could provide limitless brand exposure for your business. However, you shouldn't leave the entire job of promoting your brand to your influencer. You must also continue to ensure that you continue to add fresh and exciting content. This way, you can keep people glued to your profile after they get referred by your influencer.

3. Can enrich your content strategy

Another vital benefit of influencers is that they can enrich your TikTok content and make it more useful. If you are out of new content ideas, your influencers can help bridge the gap. If you choose an influencer who is an expert in your niche, they can produce viral content that can directly sell your products.

4. Takes the campaign to the target audience

The other great benefit you can derive from using influencers is that they your brand message to the people that need it most, which is your target audience. This is another reason why you should only recruit influencers with a following that mirrors your target audience. You would have enormous profits and returns on your investment.

5. It adds value to your audience

Content is King on TikTok, and using influencers means your marketing campaign will be carried out by experts who know what the audience wants. They are more likely to understand what your product/service is about and can communicate it to the TikTok community in an engaging way. This benefit is not just about the number of leads you generate, but the brand value you create in the minds of your prospective buyers. It also helps to build trust and reputation.

6. Boosts SEO

Because TikTok influencers make your brand more popular, this boosts your brand's search results on TikTok and search engines like Google. It makes it possible for you to rank among the top results when people search for your niche products.

7. Better results

The primary reason for choosing influencers is to achieve better results on TikTok. If you run a small business, you can partner with influencers to generate more leads, brand awareness, along with more followers, better engagement rates, and more money.

8. Makes you know your customers

When you start a business, you might have a particular target audience in mind. However, you would likely not know too much about what motivates your audience. With a TikTok influencer, you can better understand precisely what your customers expect and how to better meet their needs. How can you know this? From the comments and conversations on your influencer's post about your brand. Every time an influencer puts up a post, it attracts a lot of comments, likes, and shares. Most influencers typically respond to all the comments, including questions or comments about the brand, product, or service. You can learn a lot from this.

9. Achieve greater loyalty

Another benefit of hiring a TikTok influencer is that they are likely to produce more loyal customers. The reason is simple: people only follow and engage with an influencer they like. Similar to a loyal tribe, they are likely to stick with your brand over a longer period of time.

HOW TO CHOOSE THE RIGHT INFLUENCER

If you plan to hire a TikTok influencer to market your product, you must learn how to choose the right one. First, you must be careful to avoid fake influencers or people who bought their followers. It is usually easy to assess this. You simply go to the influencer's page and look at the performance of their videos. People with a large following but very few likes are not genuine influencers.

Furthermore, it is important to choose influencers who can

promote your brand to your target audience, so there are vital factors you must consider before choosing an influencer.

Here are some factors to consider:

1. Location

Your product/service might be location-specific. This means that it is useful for people in a particular geographical area. If you're going to hire influencers, you must look for those with appeal in your geographical region. For example, suppose you make Cake in Philadelphia. In that case, you might look to hire an influencer with lots of followers in Pennsylvania or someone with the potential to attract people in the area. You would be wasting your resources by hiring an influencer from Alaska, Toronto, or London. Because your goal is to reach your target audience, you should choose an influencer with followers from your target location.

2. Niche

Before choosing an influencer, it is also essential to assess their niche. You should look for those with similar niches to your business because they are likely to know more about your business and will be able to create viral content that can be useful for your brand. Furthermore, owing to the way TikTok's algorithm works, an influencer within your niche is more like to attract followers and likes from people who might be open to purchasing your products/service. If you use influencers that are not familiar with your niche, it might be difficult to achieve your marketing goals.

3. Age

If your products or service are targeted towards a particular age group, you must look for an influencer who is likely to attract the right audience within this age range. This is another fundamental characteristic of targeted marketing. An influencer with the wrong age group would make it unlikely to generate leads and sales from your marketing campaign.

4. Sex

If you are selling a brand/product that is dominant for a particular sex, you should select an influencer with followership or an ability to attract people of the sex. A significant example of this is cosmetics/makeup. It makes no sense to select a male sports influencer to market your mascara or lipstick.

5. Consider the engagement metrics of the influencer

Numbers are also significant when you're looking for an influencer. The most important amongst them is the engagement numbers. This includes the number of likes, comments, and shares of the influencer. Furthermore, consider the strengths and weaknesses of that influencer to help you make the correct choice. Knowing these details can help you understand whether they can reach your target audience.

6. Technical skills

Their technical skills are critical. Many people claim to be social influencers, but how many of them have the technical skill to drive the market for you? You must ascertain their talent and technical ability.

WORKING WITH MULTIPLE MICRO-INFLUENCERS

Micro-influencers are the best option if you want to reach out to a target audience with a smaller budget. Micro-influencers are TikTok users just below the rank of a full-fledged influencer.

They typically have followers from between 5 thousand to 10 thousand.

Instead of paying a single influencer to market your brand, you can instead decide to hire 3 or 4 micro-influencers with the same amount of money, who can target different locations or micro-niches to drive more traffic to your business.

Here are some of the benefits of using a micro-influencer:

- **Affordability:** Using micro-influencers is the cheapest marketing campaign available on TikTok. This is a big reason why many small businesses use them. Hiring celebrities and big influencers are remarkably expensive and might not be affordable for a teenage run startup. Many micro-influencers are not just looking for one-off payments but to secure your business for the long term. This makes them an ideal group for developing sound long-term marketing strategies that your business most definitely needs. Moreover, because they are also aspiring to grow their number of followers, they are ambitious, making them more willing to listen to you and create unique content for your brand.
- **They create genuine content:** Micro-influencers create some of the most viral content on TikTok. And their advertising content sometimes feels more genuine and natural than those of the major stars. You should use micro-influencers to create ads that don't feel like you paid someone to say what they say. It makes a difference to your potential customers, especially young people.
- **It makes content more specific:** Micro-influencers typically provide a more micro-targeted audience than any advertising group on TikTok. They enable you to place a laser focus on your specific target

market. The specifics include the age, location, niche, and interests of your target group.
- **Better to work with:** Furthermore, it is easier to work with a micro-influencer. The relationship is personalized, and you can engage with them on a less formal level. You can also establish personal connections with them and resolve issues quickly when they emerge.

HOW TO FIND AND CONTACT INFLUENCERS

There are lots of influencers on TikTok and other social media platforms. So how can you find and contact them?

The traditional method is to search your TikTok app for people successful in your business niche using long-tail-hashtags or to search among your own followers interested in your brand. However, you can also use different websites and online tools to search for the influencer you want.

Here are some of the major websites you can use:

UPFLUENCE

Upfluence is the most popular and the most used platform for finding influencers. It describes itself as the "Smartest Influencer Marketing Platform" in the world. Its database features millions of influencers from all parts of the world. If you are looking for a popular influencer and within the location you desire, you should use Upfluence.

Pros of Upfluence

- It has the largest database with more than 3 million influencers.
- It is easy and simple to use.

- It makes it easy to manage and organize your campaign.
- It is easy to monitor and measure performance.

Cons of Upfluence

- It is costly.

FANBYTES

This is another website you can use to discover and recruit TikTok influencers. You can gain access to thousands of influencers on TikTok through its website. It offers an easy-to-use user interface and provides a way to outsource your content creation to experienced TikTok users.

Pros of Fanbytes

- It makes it easy to discover top influencers.
- It makes content management and messaging possible.
- It is popular and used by top brands
- It has a very user-friendly platform

Cons of Fanbytes

- It is expensive.

INFLUENCER GRID

Influencer grid is an excellent website that functions as a database to search for leading TikTok influencers for your marketing campaign. Influencers are available in different categories and niches. It is very popular and provides a way to hire the most popular TikTok users in the world.

Pros of Influencer grid

- It is a leading influencer marketing database used by popular TikTok users.
- It is free to start – via a 7-day free trial.

Cons of Influencer grid

- Doesn't offer analytics or performance monitoring.

HEARTBEAT.COM

Heartbeat is an influencer marketing platform that connects brands with influencers to run advertising campaigns on TikTok and Instagram. It boasts one of the highest numbers of influencers on its database. It also provides mobile apps for Google and the App Store, and it makes it easy to target specific audiences for your marketing campaign, beyond standard demographics.

Pros of Heartbeat.com

- Makes it easy to scale your campaign.
- Ability to analyze the success of your campaign.
- Screens against bots and fake influencers.
- Makes it possible to target nano-influencers and micro-influencers.

Cons of Heartbeat.com

- The user interface is not the simplest to use.

GRIN

Grin is an outstanding influencer marketing software suite that can help brands find, hire, and manage influencer campaigns. It makes it possible for brands to cultivate a genuine influencer network to create a better brand image.

Pros of Grin

- Handles all payments and product deliveries to influencers.
- Provides detailed analytics.
- Provides content management.
- Used by many reputable brands
- Fully integrates into your entire marketing stack.

Cons of Grin

- You need to pay to use the software.

POPULAR PAYS

Popular Pays is a leading platform that provides a way to discover influencers, develop relationships and collaborate with them, build content, and report on performance. It makes it easy to engage in large-scale influencer marketing campaigns.

Pros of Popular Pays

- It is used by some of the world's biggest companies, including Amazon, Google, and Nike.
- Covers the entire influencer marketing process.
- Makes it easy to scale a successful campaign.

Cons

- While they provide an opportunity for startups, it is a better platform for bigger brands.

HYPERTRACE

Hypetrace is simply a database of TikTok and Instagram influencers. After subscribing, they provide access to over 400 thousand influencers and make it possible to search by location, interests, or number of followers, among others. It is not software like some of the above-mentioned tools. Neither does it provide analytics or other tools. It simply provides you with the influencer's email, making it possible for you to contact them directly.

Pros of Hypetrace

- Has a fairly large database.
- Easy to use.
- Cheaper than most of its competitors.
- Offers a free "Lite" plan.

Cons of Hypetrace

- Does not offer analytics.
- Does not cover the entire influencer marketing lifecycle.

TIPS FOR CONTACTING AND NEGOTIATING WITH INFLUENCERS

Tips for contacting TikTok influencers

- Follow and engage with them on Instagram about 2-3 weeks before you begin your outreach (Ho, 2019).
- First message: send them your name, company name, and ask if they're interested in a paid collaboration with you (Ho, 2019).
- If you get a response, send them the following:
- Precisely what you want from them.
- Your budget.
- What kinds of benefits you are willing to offer, like free membership (Trösch, 2020).
- What you want them to say in the ads about the values of your product.
- Give the influencers the freedom to do their own thing (Ho, 2019) (Payne, 2020).

Negotiating and Agreeing on terms with TikTok influencers

- Provide clear instructions and set the price.
- Don't give them a script. Let them use their own words.
- Send them a link to a folder where they can drop the videos.
- Remind them to use #ad or #sponsored.
- Send them examples, so they know precisely what you're looking for.
- Tell them to record their videos outside the TikTok app, so they don't contain a watermark.

- Tell them they'll get paid within 24-48 hours after delivering the content.
- Tell them what payment system you're going to use and ask for their details.

(Appelt, 2019)

HIRING A GOOD VIDEO EDITOR ON UPWORK TO CREATE GOOD AD CONTENT

Chapter 2 extensively covered everything you need to know about hiring freelancers.

However, if you're looking to succeed more with your influencer campaigns, you can hire a video editor to make the videos for your influencer marketing campaigns. You can easily hire from places like Upwork.com, Fiverr.com, and 99designs. You can ask the video editor to create 15 videos from 3 videos that you provide.

There are many video editors on these platforms who can save you a lot of time and effort. Therefore, before choosing a freelancer, you should look for those with experience in editing videos. Take your time to read the freelancer's reviews and make sure they have a history of completing tasks with excellence. Moreover, these freelance websites typically provide some protection for the buyer/client. This means you do not pay or approve a project until you are fully satisfied with it.

CONCLUSION

"You miss 100% of the shots you don't take."

— WAYNE GRETZKY

The first chapter of this book defined the history of TikTok and the reasons for its popularity. It also explained why you should care about bringing your business to TikTok. The first reason is that TikTok currently provides the best marketing opportunity in the world. And many people like – Fitz and the Tantrums and Lil Nas X – have used it to achieve remarkable successes. Other reasons you should get on TikTok are its 1 billion users and its users' unique content and talents. Chapter 1 concludes by explaining the importance of hashtags, timing, authenticity, and TikTok's *For You* page.

The second chapter explains everything about creating a perfect TikTok profile. It provided detailed explanations about how to download and register your TikTok account, how to choose a good username, how to write a world-class bio and the types of bio you can have. It also touched on how you can link your other social media accounts – like YouTube and Instagram

– to TikTok and how you can add your website or online store to your account.

Chapter 3 delved into TikTok content creation and how you can create amazing videos on TikTok. It explained issues like the types of videos you can create, how to add sounds and effects to your posts, and how to participate in the latest challenges and trends using relevant hashtags. It also explains how to select the best cameras and how to buy cheap lighting to make your videos more appealing.

Chapter 4 began to explore how to grow your account. It provided a detailed breakdown of how you can create a content plan and its importance to your success on TikTok. Aspects of the content plan like the content calendar, how to research your target audience, setting your marketing goals, and measuring your success and ROI were also explained. A good ROI on TikTok means you made more money than you spent on promoting your content. The book also explained the concept of "cross-promoting" videos and posts. This is the idea of promoting your TikTok videos on your other social media platforms like your Twitter, WhatsApp status, Instagram, and Snapchat, among others. The chapter ends by explaining how to engage with other TikTok users.

Chapter 5 explains how you can register for a free TikTok pro account, which would provide you with a detailed data analysis of your engagement on TikTok, including the number of new followers you get and your posts' performance. TikTok pro would provide you data like the number of views on your videos, the number of shares it received, and the location/gender breakdown of your video viewers. The chapter ends by providing details on how to have a verified account on TikTok and future innovations you can expect from TikTok.

Chapter 6 covered everything about TikTok ads, explaining concepts like *in-feed ads, brand takeover ads, top-view ads,* and *branded hashtag challenges.* Branded hashtag challenges are the most expensive type of TikTok ads, enabling brands to sponsor a hashtag/trend and have the TikTok community participate. It is a way to achieve maximum exposure for your brand. The chapter also provided a step by step guide on setting up your ad account on TikTok and how to measure/analyze an ad's success or failure. Finally, chapter 6 concludes by exploring everything about the TikTok ads manager.

The final chapter – Chapter 7 explains how to take advantage of TikTok influencers and all the benefits it can bring to your business. It explains the financial advantage an influencer provides, compared with paying directly for TikTok ads. It also explains the importance of choosing only influencers with the right audience for the brand. The chapter goes on to explain the concept of micro-influencers and why they provide the cheapest way to reach a lot of TikTok users. Micro-influencers are TikTok users with about 5000 to 10000 followers. Because they cost between $20-$50 for a post, they provide an unrivaled Return on Investment and an easy way to grow your brand. The chapter ends by providing a detailed guide on how to hire influencers, contact them, chat with them, and negotiate their pay.

Now that you have all the tools you need, you need to go out there and use them. As Joe Sabah once said, "you don't have to be great to start, but you have to start to be great." There is no better encouragement I can give you to begin your business. It is normal to have some doubts before you begin. You might look at other successful young girls on TikTok and wonder if you can attain those heights. My answer is, you will never know how far you can go if you don't try. You have to begin somewhere and follow all the steps highlighted in this book. You certainly wouldn't become an overnight success, but if you are well prepared, creative, and smart about your approach, you certainly have a shot. Additionally, TikTok remains a free app, and it'll literally cost you nothing to begin.

You don't have a professional camera? Use your phone's camera. You don't have a good voice? Use the millions of sound clips on TikTok. You don't have money for ads? Talk to your friends/family about your business and ask them to promote you on their posts. If 10 of your friends with 100-200 followers put up a post about your business, it'll get seen by thousands of people. Nothing should stop you from pursuing your dreams. All you need is your business idea and the motivation to keep it running.

ALSO BY ANASTASIA OLSON

This book will help you:

- Find the business idea that will suit your personality.
- Do market research and select the best marketing strategies that will suit your business.
- Know how to keep your business in the long run.

https://www.amazon.com/gp/product/B08JDXBT1F

We are so happy that you have finished reading our book, and *we are working hard to write higher quality books for you through your feedback! Visit the link and leave us your feedback:*

https://www.amazon.com/review/create-review/?asin=B08NKBS5GX

Thank you so much for takingtime out of your day, we appreciate you!

11 SUPRISING HACKS TO GROW YOUR BRAND ON TIKTOK

(NEVER START A TIKTOK WITHOUT THIS...)

To receive those steps, visit the link:

http://book2climb.com/TikTokSuprisingHacks

REFERENCES

Adan Kohnhorst. "TikTok Has a New Video Search Function From the Future." RADII | Culture, Innovation, and Life in Today's China, 26 Sept. 2019, www.radiichina.com/tiktok-new-video-search-function-is-from-the-future/

AdEspresso. "A/B Testing | A Beginners Guide to Split Testing Facebook Ads in 2017." AdEspresso, www.adespresso.com/guides/facebook-ads-optimization/ab-testing/

Alexander, J., 2020. Tiktok Reveals Some Of The Secrets, And Blind Spots, Of Its Recommendation Algorithm. [online] The Verge. Available at: https://www.theverge.com/2020/6/18/21296044/tiktok-for-you-page-algorithm-sides-engagement-data-creators-trends-sounds

An, Mimi. "Content Trends: Preferences Emerge Along Generational Fault Lines." Hubspot.Com, 2017, blog.hubspot.com/marketing/content-trends-preferences.
Appelt, Diana. "Successfully Negotiating Terms With Influencer Marketers." Www.Captevrix.Com, 2019, www.captevrix.-

com/news/successfully-negotiating-terms-with-influencer-marketers. Accessed 20 Oct. 2020.

Bern, Fabian. "What TikTok's Chinese Predecessor Douyin Can Reveal about Its Future." The Next Web, 2 Mar. 2019, www.thenextweb.com/contributors/2019/03/02/tiktok-chinese-predecessor-douyin-reveal-about-its-future/

Boost, Creative. "How To Build A TikTok Marketing Strategy For Your Business." Creative Boost, 17 Mar. 2020, creative-boost-.net/how-to-build-a-tik-tok-marketing-strategy/. Borak, Masha. "Movie Streaming on TikTok." South China Morning Post, 1 Apr. 2020, www.scmp.com/abacus/culture/article/3077820/chinas-tiktok-turning-movie-streaming-platform

Brown A., 2020. TikTok's 7 Highest Earning Stars: New Forbes List Led by Teen Queens Addison Rae and Charli D'Armelio. [online] Available at: www.forbes .com/sites/abrambrown/2020/08/06/tik-toks-highest-earning-stars-teen-queens-addison-rae-and-charli-damelio-rule/#39ec050d5087

Carless, S. (2020) Game Discoverability: To Demo, Or Not To Demo. [online] Gamasutra. Available at: https://www.gamasutra.com/blogs/SimonCarless/20200406/360754/Game_discoverability_to_demo_or_not_to_demo.phphttps://twitter.com/ZombiesRunGame/status/1247074858003038210

Celebrity Access (2019) The Tiktok Algorithm: How It Works. [online] Available at: https://celebrityaccess.com/2019/11/07/hype-bot-the-tiktok-algorithm-how-it-works/
Connor. "How To Get a Verified Checkmark (Formerly Crown) in TikTok." Tech Junkie, 30 July 2020, www.social.techjunkie.-com/get-crown-tiktok/#:~:text=How%20Do%20I%20Get%20Verified%20in%20TikTok%3F%201 .
Consult Ease Edutech (2020). Things You Need To Know About

Tiktok. [online] Available at: https://consulteaseedutech.-com/2020/05/30/things-you-need-to-know-about-tiktok/?share=email
Crumpley, Joshua. "TikTok: How to Get A Verified Account Badge." ScreenRant, 22 July 2020, screenrant.com/tiktok-verified-accounts-badge-requirements-explained/.

Don, Ron. "The Ultimate Guide to TikTok Advertising." Visiture, 14 Feb. 2020, www.visiture.com/blog/tiktok-advertising-an-ultimate-guide-to-advertising-on-tiktok/

Elama. "How to Advertise on TikTok: Step by Step Guide." ELama | Knowledge Base, www.help.elama.global/hc/en-us/articles/360011708820-How-to-Advertise-on-TikTok-Step-by-Step-Guide

Facebook. "Guide to the Learning Phase." Facebook for Business, www.facebook.com/business/m/one-sheeters/guide-to-the-learning-phase

Fasulo, Alexandra. "5 Ways to Grow Your TikTok Following in Just One Month." Business 2 Community, 2020, www.business2community.com/social-media/5-ways-to-grow-your-tiktok-following-in-just-one-month-02310966. Accessed 20 Oct. 2020.

Fedotoff, Alex. "Ultimate Guide on Scaling Facebook Ad Campaigns." Facebook Ad Agency & Consultant | Alex Fedotoff, www.alexfedotoff.com/scaling-facebook-ads/

Financial, Times. "How to Become TikTok Famous." Www.Ft.-Com, 2019, www.ft.com/content/dd7234e8-fcb9-11e9-98fd-4d6c20050229

Grill, Chipotle Mexican. "Chipotle Gives Reins To Biggest TikTok Creators To Disrupt Traditional Big Game Advertising At Every Timeout." Www.Prnewswire.Com, 30 Jan. 2020, www.

prnewswire.com/news-releases/chipotle-gives-reins-to-biggest-tiktok-creators-to-disrupt-traditional-big-game-advertising-at-every-timeout-300995917.html

Gupta, Prahka. "To Kill or Not to Kill Your Facebook Campaign: 15 Reasons Why." The Startup, 28 July 2019, www.medium.com/swlh/to-kill-or-not-to-kill-your-facebook-campaign-15-reasons-why-67f7b96ac53d

Goldkorn, Jeremy. "The Difference between TikTok and Douyin." SupChina, 25 Sept. 2019, www.supchina.com/2019/09/25/the-difference-between-tiktok-and-douyin/

Hills, M. (2020). Best celebrities to follow on TikTok, from Miley to Lewis Capaldi. Evening Standard. from https://www.standard.co.uk/insider/alist/celebrities-on-tiktok-including-bts-lewis-capaldi-will-smith-and-miley-cyrus-a4279366.html

Ho, Leslie. "How to Contact Instagram Influencers: The Perfect Process for 2020." Inzpire.Me Blog, 6 Dec. 2019, blog.inzpire.me/how-to-contact-instagram-influencers/#Step_3_Engage_with_influencers_on_social_media. Accessed 20 Oct. 2020

Houghton, B., 2019. The Tiktok Algorithm: How It Works. [online] Hypebot. Available at: https://www.hypebot.com/hypebot/2019/11/the-tiktok-algorithm-how-it-works.html

Hutchinson, Andrew. "TikTok Adds 'Gamified Brand Effect' Templates to Help Businesses Create More Engaging Promotions." Social Media Today, 22 July 2020, www.socialmediatoday.com/news/tiktok-adds-gamified-brand-effect-templates-to-help-businesses-create-mor/582145/

Influencer Marketing Hub. (2020a). Tiktok Money Calculator

[Influencer Engagement & Earnings Estimator]. [online] Available at: <https://influencermarketinghub.com/tiktok-money-calculator/

Influencer Marketing Hub (2020b) 50 Tiktok Stats That Will Blow Your Mind In 2020 [UPDATED]. [online] Available at: https://influencermarketinghub.com/tiktok-stats/

Influencer Magazine, Hub. "4 of the Best TikTok Scheduling Tools (+ How to Schedule TikTok Posts)." Influencer Marketing Hub, 20 May 2020, influencermarketinghub.com/tiktok-scheduling-tools/. Accessed 20 Oct. 2020.

Influencer Marketing, Hub. "Your Ultimate Guide to TikTok Hashtags | Increase Your TikTok Post Reach." Influencer Marketing Hub, 22 Jan. 2020, influencermarketinghub.com/tiktok-hashtags/#:~:text=Another%20way%20to%20look%20for

Influencer Marketing Hub. "How Does Advertising on TikTok Work?" Influencer Marketing Hub, 3 Jan. 2020, www.influencermarketinghub.com/advertising-on-tiktok/

Jessica Worb. "Everything You Need to Know About TikTok Ads." Later Blog, 12 June 2020, www.later.com/blog/tiktok-ads/

John, Steven. "How to Trim a TikTok Video in 2 Ways, and Make Precise Edits to Your Videos." Business Insider, 2020, www.businessinsider.com/how-to-trim-tik-tok-video?r=US&IR=T

Kotlyar, Brian. "Customer Acquisition Cost (CAC): How to Calculate CAC and Reduce Cost." Inside Intercom, 7 Nov. 2018, www.intercom.com/blog/what-is-customer-acquisition-cost/

Kramer, Roderick. "Rethinking Trust." Harvard Business Review, Aug. 2014, www.hbr.org/2009/06/rethinking-trust

Lachlan Kirkwood. "TikTok Analytics: What Marketers Need to Know." Social Media Marketing | Social Media Examiner, 15 Oct. 2019, www.socialmediaexaminer.com/tiktok-analytics-what-marketers-need-to-know/

Lacombe, Gabriella. Guess Launches Sponsored Fashion Challenge in Partnership with Video App TikTok. 4 Sept. 2018, www.us.fashionnetwork.com/news/Guess-launches-sponsored-fashion-challenge-in-partnership-with-video-app-tiktok,1009433.html

Later Media. "TikTok Analytics: Your Guide to Understanding the Metrics." Later Blog, 13 May 2020, www.later.com/blog/tiktok-analytics/

Leskin, P. (2020). Charli D'Amelio has taken over as TikTok's biggest star. These are the 40 most popular creators on the viral video app. Business Insider. Retrieved October 13, 2020, from https://www.businessinsider.com/tiktok-most-popular-stars-gen-z-influencers-social-media-app-2019-6?r=US&IR=T

Lister, Mary. "5 Simple Steps to Set Up Your TikTok Ads." Www.-Wordstream.Com, 15 Aug. 2020, www.wordstream.com/blog/ws/2020/07/22/tiktok-ads

Maddala, Sekhar. "TikTok Starts Offering Full-Length Feature Films Through Popular Video App Douyin in China." Indiashopps News, 1 Apr. 2020, www.indiashopps.com/news/tik-tok-offering-full-length-feature-films-douyin-china/

Martinez, Tara. "Here's What To Know About BLACKPINK, The First K-Pop Girl Group To Perform At Coachella." Elite Daily, 2019, www.elitedaily.com/p/who-is-blackpink-theyre-the-first-k-pop-girl-group-to-perform-at-coachella-its-obvious-why-15648883

McGlew, M. (2020) This Is How The Tiktok Algorithm Works.

[online] Later. Available at: https://later.com/blog/tiktok-algorithm/ https://later.com/blog/tiktok-hashtags/https://later.com/blog/tiktok-algorithm/

Mishra, Rajesh. "How to Get Verified Badge on TikTok in 2020." Beebom, 19 May 2020, www.beebom.com/how-get-verified-tiktok/

Mohsin, M. (2020) 10 TIKTOK STATISTICS THAT YOU NEED TO KNOW IN 2020 [INFOGRAPHIC]. [online] Oberlo. Available at: <https://www.oberlo.com/blog/tiktok-statistics>

Pasley, Mike. "Kill It, Keep It, or Scale It?" Viralstyle Sellers, 28 Mar. 2017, www.sellers.viralstyle.com/blog/kill-it-keep-it-or-scale-it/

Payne, Kevin. "How to Work With Influencers on TikTok." Socialbakers, 6 Apr. 2020, www.socialbakers.com/blog/how-to-work-with-influencers-on-tiktok. Accessed 13 Apr. 2020

Perez, Sarah. "TikTok's New 'Hashtag Challenge Plus' Lets Video Viewers Shop for Products in the App." TechCrunch, Oct. 2019, www.techcrunch.com/2019/08/19/tiktoks-new-hashtag-challenge-plus-lets-video-viewers-shop-for-products-in-the-app /

Poniewozik J., Hess A., Caramanica J., Kourlas G., Morris W., (2019) 48 Hours in the Strange and Beautiful World of TikTok [online] Available at: https://www.nytimes.com/interactive/2019/10/10/arts/TIK-TOK.html

Previte, Jeff. 6 Examples of Brands Crushing the TikTok Marketing Game (+ Tips). 27 Jan. 2020, www.business2community.com/social-media/6-examples-of-brands-crushing-the-tiktok-marketing-game-tips-02278523

Rijo, Daniel. "PPC Land." Ppcland.Substack.Com, 2020, www.ppc.land/tiktok-launches-pro-accounts-offering-new-insights-to-creators/#:~:text=What%20is%20a%20pro%20account

Sandoval, Daniel. "Spy on Your Competitor's Facebook and Instagram Ads [2020]." Www.Digitalassembly.Agency, 21 Jan. 2020, www.digitalassembly.agency/spy-on-competitors-facebook-instagram-ads-with-facebook-ad-library/

Sharma, Rhimzim. "TikTok Pro Account: What Is It? How to Get One?" Systweak Software, 18 Oct. 2019, www.blogs.systweak.com/tiktok-pro-account/

Shaw L., (2020) TikTOk is the new music kingmaker, and labels want to get paid [online]. Available at https://www.bloomberg.-com/news/articles/2019-05-10/tiktok-is-the-new-music-kingmaker-and-labels-want-to-get-paid
SHEREEN, COOKING with. "COOKING with SHEREEN (@cookingwithshereen) Official TikTok | Watch COOKING with SHEREEN's Newest TikTok Videos." TikTok, 2020, www.tiktok.com/@cookingwithshereen

Singh, Manish. "TikTok Tests Social Commerce." TechCrunch, Dec. 2019, www.techcrunch.com/2019/11/15/tiktok-link-bio-social-commerce/#:~:text=TikTok%20is%20beginning%20to%20dabble%20in%20social%20commerce

Smart, Insights. "Content Marketing Strategy - Smart Insights Digital Marketing." Smart Insights, 2011, www.smartinsights.com/content-management/content-marketing-strategy/

Social Media Examiner. "How to Use TikTok Challenges for Business." Social Media Examiner | Social Media Marketing, 25 Feb. 2020, www.socialmediaexaminer.com/how-to-use-tiktok-challenges-for-business/

Social, Triggers. "The 80/20 Rule for Building a Blog Audience." Social Triggers, 2013, socialtriggers.com/80-20-blog-building/. Accessed 20 Oct. 2020.

StayHipp. "A Guide to Trends on TikTok." StayHipp, 13 May 2019, stayhipp.com/guides/a-guide-to-trends-on-tiktok/

Strapagiel L., (2020) How TikTok Made "Old Town Road" Become Both A Meme and a Banger. [online] Buzzfeed news. Available at: https://www.buzzfeednews.com/article/laurenstrapagiel/tiktok-lil-nas-x-old-town-road

Trösch, Daniel. "How to Negotiate with Influencers in 6 Steps." Fourstarzz Media, 20 Apr. 2020, www.fourstarzz.com/post/how-to-negotiate-with-influencers. Accessed 20 Oct. 2020.

Taulli T., (2020). [online] Forbes. Available at http://www.forbes.com/sites/tomtaulli/2020/01/31/tiktok-why-the-enormous-successs/TikTok

TeeSpring Community. "How Do You Know When to Scale an Ad and When to Kill It?" Teespring Community, www.community.teespring.com/training-center/how-do-you-know-when-to-scale-an-ad-and-when-to-kill-it/

TikTok (2020). How Tiktok Recommends Videos #Foryou. [online] Available at: https://newsroom.tiktok.com/en-us/how-tiktok-recommends-videos-for-you

TikTok (2020) TikTok Marketing Partners [online] Available at: www.ads.tiktok.com/marketing-partners.
TikTok. "About Lookalike Audience." Ads.Tiktok.Com, www.ads.tiktok.com/help/article?aid=6746381707865227270

TikTok. "Automated Creative Optimization." Ads.Tiktok.Com, www.ads.tiktok.com/help/article?aid=6670043695674294277

TikTok. "Create and Manage Reports." Ads.Tiktok.Com, www.ads.tiktok.com/help/article?aid=6701858262603530245

TikTok. "Create Lookalike Audience." Ads.Tiktok.Com, www.ads.tiktok.com/help/article?aid=6746382866076139525

TikTok. "Interest Targeting." Ads.Tiktok.Com, www.ads.tiktok.com/help/article?aid=6730493704647213061

TikTok. "Learning Phase." Ads.Tiktok.Com, www.ads.tiktok.com/help/article?aid=7538785998242902O3

TikTok. "Set up an Ad Group." Ads.Tiktok.Com, www.ads.tiktok.com/help/article?aid=6669731941937315845

TikTok. "TikTok Ads Structure." Ads.Tiktok.Com, www.ads.tiktok.com/help/article?aid=6669376375121510405

Vrinda Singh. "How to Advertise on TikTok." Social Media Marketing | Social Media Examiner, 30 Oct. 2019, www.socialmediaexaminer.com/how-to-advertise-tiktok/

Wiltshire, E. (2019, October 24). SMT Expert Roundup: The Future of TikTok. Social Media Today. https://www.socialmediatoday.com/news/smt-expert-roundup-the-future-of-tiktok/565714/

Wired (2020) How The 'For You' Algorithm Works. [online] Available at: https://www.wired.com/story/tiktok-finally-explains-for-you-algorithm-works/

Ye, Josh. "Nine National Museums Host Virtual Tours on China's TikTok." Abacus, 21 Feb. 2020, www.abacusnews.com/china-tech-city/nine-national-museums-host-virtual-tours-chinas-tiktok/article/3051698 .

Printed in Great Britain
by Amazon

32940467R00086